Copenhagen

CULT RECIPES

Christine Rudolph & Susie Theodorou

Copenhagen

CULT RECIPES

Photography **Christine Rudolph**
Illustration **Tusnelda Sommers**

murdoch books
Sydney | London

CONTENTS

Introduction

Food is taken seriously in Copenhagen, and the locals have many opinions on traditional preparations and how it's served. It is New Nordic cuisine from about 2005, however, that has helped put Copenhagen on the map as a dining destination. This cuisine is about using and producing traditional foods that are locally grown. It's about keeping recipes simple and tasty. No matter how big or small the restaurant, chefs care about the ingredients they use, creating close ties with producers and keeping menus seasonal. Home cooks are also respectful of ingredients – simple herbs and greens grown on rooftops and window boxes, and small vegetable patches can be found everywhere.

All this love of food and eating exaggerates that 'hygge' (cosy) atmosphere, which can be found all over Copenhagen. There are large shared tables in restaurants, while outside eating is encouraged with large communal tables in public places. You can walk through some of the old narrow cobbled streets and find an old classic smørrebrød place. Or rent a bike and go out to the up-and-coming areas to try some of the new casual restaurants, where you eat simple local produce while relaxing on old classic Børge Mogensen chairs and stripped-back reclaimed wooden tables.

BREAKFAST

A day in Copehagen traditionally begins with three ingredients: rye bread, eggs and coffee. Now, however, it has become fashionable to eat freshly baked crisp pastries from the artisanal bakeries that are scattered around the city (you have to be quick, though — they sell out early). This chapter includes breads and pastries, such as cinnamon or cardamom buns, which have been adapted for home cooks, as well as breakfasts for lazy days, including porridge with various toppings and breakfast plates with smoked meat and fish.

35 kr.	Kaffekombucha	kr.
40 kr.	Kaffe-softice	30 kr.
45 kr.	Varm Chokolade	40 kr.

THE COFFEE

fee Pick-up ↓

THE COFFEE COLLECTIVE

Sourdough rye bread is found everywhere in Copenhagen. It takes while to make, though, so it's a true labour of love. After baking, leave the bread for a day before slicing it very thinly. To store it, wrap it in paper towels, then a tea towel, and it will keep for a week.

RUGBRØD
rye bread

Makes a 1kg loaf ▪ Preparation: 2 days ▪ Cooking: 1½–2 hours

Ingredients

80 g raw sunflower seeds
80 g raw pumpkin seeds
40 g raw flaxseeds

LEVAIN
50 g hydrated sourdough starter (buy online)
100 g rye flour

DOUGH
75 ml dark beer such as stout,
   at room temperature
190 g rye flour
150 g wholegrain rye flour
150 g wholegrain spelt flour
15 g fine sea salt
7 g barley malt syrup
2 tbsp rye flakes, for topping

Preheat the oven to 180°C (350°F). Toast the seeds for 8–10 minutes until just toasted. Cool, place in a bowl, cover with water and soak overnight.

For the levain, put the starter, rye flour and 100 ml room temperature water in a bowl, mix well and cover. Leave overnight (at 22–23°C/72-73°F) or at least 12 hours to ferment.

The next day, drain the seeds and pat dry on kitchen paper. Place the levain in a bowl and gradually stir in the beer and 500ml (2 cups) room temperature water to dissolve the levain. Add all the dry ingredients, including the seeds and the barley malt syrup. Mix well. Cover and leave in a warm place for 1½–2 hours.

Preheat the oven to 200°C (400°F). Place the dough in a 1kg loaf pan or 2 smaller ones. Sprinkle the rye flakes on top, then place on a baking tray and bake for 30 minutes. Reduce the oven temperature to 180°C (350°F) and bake for 1½ hours. Once done, cool completely.

Coffee

The coffee culture has exploded in the last decade in Copenhagen, even though the Danish already have a history of being a big coffee nation. Coffee drinking is now a social event, and the city has seen a huge increase of hip, welcoming and very stylish coffee bars.

There are several different methods to brewing coffee including hand-brew or pour-over, tude cortado (also known as cortado), latte, cappuccino or Americano.

Espresso: a single shot of espresso (about 25 ml shot of coffee).

Cortado: espresso served in an espresso cup topped with steamed milk and a touch of froth.

Macchiato: espresso served in an espresso cup topped with the froth of steamed milk.

Cappuccino: espresso made with 25 ml coffee and topped with 75–85ml steamed foamy milk.

Latte: milky coffee made with 50 ml espresso topped with 175 ml steamed milk, not necessarily frothy.

Pour-over: grind 30 g coffee beans to a mixture similar to sea salt. Line a single filter with a paper filter and add the coffee. Level the surface. Place over a 250 ml serving cup. Boil 600 ml water to 95°C (203°F), then gradually pour the water over the coffee in 3 stages, each time waiting for the water to filter through into the cup. Serve with or without milk.

Iced coffee: most often this is filter coffee cooled quickly. Serve over ice with or without milk.

Cappuccino

Iced coffee

Pour-over

Latte

Tea

Even though Denmark is a nation of coffee lovers, natural, herbal teas are also popular. To make a cup of herbal tea, place your chosen herb or mixture of herbs in a pot or cup, pour over freshly boiled water and leave the herbs to steep for 3–5 minutes, then strain and serve, sweetened with honey, if liked.

Hops: hops are good for relieving different forms of stress. Steep 2–3 hop clusters in just-boiled water for 3–5 minutes. Strain or leave in the water. Sweeten with honey, if liked.

Tarragon: steeped tarragon leaves aids digestion, helps with water retention as well as having a relaxing effect on the body. Tear leaves from 2 sprigs and steep in 300 ml hot water for 10 minutes.

Rosehip: rosehips are a great antioxidant. To make tea, trim the rosehips (bulbs) and cut in half. Scoop out the seeds and discard. Steep 6–8 rosehip bulbs in 300 ml water for 10 minutes. Strain and sweeten with honey, if liked.

Lemon verbena: this herb is an antioxidant, aids digestion, calms the stomach and is good for anxiety. Fresh lemon verbena and mint are a good combination as well. Steep a lemon verbena sprig in hot water for 2–3 minutes. Serve warm or cold.

Mountain sage: this popular tea, imported from the Greek Islands, is served in many high-end tea shops. Steep the leaves in hot water for 5–8 minutes then serve. As well as helping to prevent digestive problems, it has been found to help with depression.

Juno, a popular bakery, makes some of the best rustic breads in the city. The baker and pastry chef, Emil Glazer, is an ex-Noma chef and has kindly shared this recipe. You will need to cultivate the sourdough starter, which you can buy online or in healthfood stores.

MORGENFORM
morning bread

Makes 1kg loaf ▪ Preparation: 3 hours over 2 days ▪ Cooking: 40 minutes

Ingredients

125 g sourdough starter (buy online)

175 g sifted strong bread flour,
   plus extra for dusting

75 g wholegrain rye flour

100 g wholegrain einkorn flour

11 g salt

Day 1

Mix 325 ml (30–35°C/86–95°F) warm water, the starter and flours together. Rest for 30 minutes.

Mix the dough for 15 minutes until smooth and elastic, then add the salt and mix for 2–3 minutes. Put the dough into a lightly oiled bowl, cover and leave at room temperature for 20 minutes, then fold the dough over itself and repeat every 30 minutes for 2 hours.

Shape the dough into an oval on a floured surface. Place in a greased 1kg loaf tin and leave for about 30–60 minutes. Chill overnight.

Day 2

Preheat the oven to 250°C (475°F). Allow the dough to come to room temperature (about 15 minutes).

Dust the top of the dough with flour, then make a deep cut on the surface. Bake in the bottom of the oven for 40 minutes, or until the bread feels hollow when tapped on the base. Cool for 10 minutes, then remove the bread from the tin and leave on a wire rack until cooled. Slice and serve with butter.

Juno bakery also shared this recipe for traditional crackers, which are common in Copenhagen. They roll the dough out into large thin 25cm round discs, then cut out a small hole from the centre with a 5cm cookie cutter. You can also make rectangles or ovals.

KNÆKBRØD
crackers

Makes 10 large crackers ▪ Preparation: 2 hours over 2 days ▪ Cooking: about 1 hour

Ingredients

100 g sourdough starter (buy online)

100 g (⅔ cup) wholegrain øland wheat flour
   (ølandshvedemel or wholegrain flour)

100 g (⅔ cup) sifted strong bread flour

30 g wholegrain rye flour

1 g fresh yeast

6 g salt

Day 1

Mix all the ingredients together with 100ml water until it's a firm dough. Place the dough in a container with a tight-fitting lid, cover and leave to rest until the next day.

Day 2

Preheat the oven to its hottest, 250°C (475°F) or 280°C (540°F). Divide the dough into 40 g pieces. Roll out each piece into your desired shape on a lightly floured surface, about 2mm thin. Place on baking paper and bake in batches for 3–5 minutes until dark golden brown. Rest on a wire rack until cold and crisp.

Boiled eggs and toast are top of the breakfast list in most homes, but they are also served in cafés and coffee shops. Usually the eggs are served in egg cups; most homes and cafés have a collection. It doesn't matter if they don't match – it's part of the hygge feeling.

THE BOILED EGG

Serves 4 ▪ Preparation: 2 minutes ▪ Cooking: 5–9 minutes

Ingredients
4 large organic eggs, at room temperature

Bring a small-medium pot of water to the boil, then reduce to a gentle simmer. Lower the eggs into the water, stir and start the timer. As soon as the eggs are done, remove and run under cold water. Serve.

5 minutes

Very runny yolk
Perfect for eating in the shell and dipping with toast.

6 minutes

Set white & runny yolk
Good for eating in the shell and dipping with toast.

7 minutes

Set white, sticky yolk
Perfect for an egg and bacon sandwich.

8 minutes

Soft set yolk
Good for serving with salads and some smørrebrød.

9 minutes

Hard-boiled
Excellent for slicing and chopping for smørrebrød.

Lovage, also known as sea parsley, is a herb that tastes of celery. Since it is strong-tasting it can be mixed with parsley so that the finished dish is not too intense.

FRIED EGG
with lovage pesto

Serves 4 ▪ Preparation: 25 minutes ▪ Cooking: 5–8 minutes

Ingredients

PESTO

100 g flat-leaf parsley, separated into small sprigs

50 g lovage (or celery leaves), plus sprigs
   to garnish

50 g pecorino cheese, roughly grated

100 g toasted walnuts, roughly chopped

200 ml grapeseed or extra virgin olive oil

1 lemon

TO ASSEMBLE

1–2 tbsp grapeseed or extra virgin olive
   oil or salted butter, for frying

4 large organic eggs

4 slices thick sourdough bread, lightly toasted

Make the pesto. Blanch the herbs in a pot of boiling water for 30 seconds. Scoop out and cool in ice-cold water. Drain and squeeze dry in a tea towel, then add to a food processor with the cheese and walnuts and blitz for 10 seconds. Start to add the oil and process to a rough texture. If you want it runnier, add a little more oil while the processor is running. Taste and add a squeeze of lemon juice and salt and black pepper.

Heat a little oil or butter in a frying pan for 30 seconds, then swirl around to coat the base of the pan. Crack each egg into the pan and fry to your liking.

Place the toast on a serving plate, spread with pesto and top with a fried egg. Or serve the toast on the side of the pesto and fried eggs. Garnish with a sprig of lovage to serve.

WIENERBRØD
plaited fruit danish

Serves 8 ▪ Preparation: 1 hour 45 minutes, plus 1½ hours rising ▪ Cooking: 30–40 minutes

Ingredients

BASIC DANISH PASTRY DOUGH

150 ml milk

50 g sugar

1 tsp salt

250 g (1⅔ cups) strong white bread flour

250 g (1⅔ cups) plain flour or pastry flour

7 g (2 tsp) dried yeast

1 medium egg

250g lightly salted butter, cut into 8 slices,
   firm but not cold

FILLING & TOPPING

225g puréed apples (p.38)

225g apples, peeled and sliced about 1cm thick

100g almonds or pecans, chopped

2 tbsp soft brown sugar

1 egg yolk beaten with 2 tbsp milk

Gently heat the milk, sugar and salt. Combine the flours and yeast in a stand mixer fitted with the dough hook. Pour in the milk, then the egg and knead for 1–2 minutes, adding 1–2 tbsp flour if needed. Leave the dough in an oiled bowl in a warm place for 1 hour.

Roll the dough out to a large rectangle, 1 cm thick, with the short side facing you, then arrange the butter slices in the centre third, from left to right. Fold the left third of the dough over the butter, then right third of dough to enclose. Seal the edges. Turn the dough 90° clockwise and roll out to a 50 x 30 cm rectangle. Fold in three as before. Cover and chill for 15 minutes. Repeat 3 more times.

Roll the dough out to a 50 x 30cm rectangle. With the short side facing you, spread the puréed apples from top to bottom, in the centre third of the dough. Arrange the sliced apples on top. Mix the nuts and sugar together and set aside.

Cut the pastry either side of the filling into 2.5 cm-wide strips, leaving them attached at the centre, close to the filling. Brush the pastry with water, then plait the dough so that the filling is covered. Rest in a warm place for 30 minutes.

Preheat the oven to 180°C (350°F). Brush the pastry with egg wash, then sprinkle over the nut mix. Bake for 30–40 minutes until risen and golden. Cool.

In Denmark this traditional yeast-based dough is flavoured with cinnamon, while in Sweden it's flavoured with cardamom. The current trend in Copenhagen, however, is to eat these flavoured with cardamom.

KANELSNURRE
cinnamon buns

Makes 12 buns ▪ Preparation: 1 hour, plus 2½ hours proving ▪ Cooking: 25–30 minutes

Ingredients

350 ml whole milk

2 cinnamon sticks or 6 cardamom
   pods, roughly crushed to just reveal
   the black seeds

200 g unsalted butter, diced

500 g (3⅓ cups) strong white bread flour

7 g (2 tsp) dried yeast

½ tsp salt

225 g sugar

2 tbsp ground cinnamon or cardamom

2 tsp sunflower oil, for oiling

1 egg yolk beaten with 2 tbsp milk,
   to glaze

2–3 tbsp pearl sugar

Gently heat the milk, cinnamon sticks and 50 g of the butter. Combine the flour, yeast, salt, 75 g of the sugar, and 1 tsp ground cinnamon in a stand mixer fitted with the dough hook. Remove the spice from the milk and, with the motor running, gradually mix into the flour. Knead the dough until smooth, then put into an oiled bowl and turn until coated with oil. Cover and leave in a warm place until doubled in size.

Make the spiced sugar. Mix the remaining spice with the remaining sugar. Reserve 3 tbsp, then mix the rest of the spiced sugar with the remaining butter.

Knock back the dough and roll out to a 35 x 45 cm rectangle on a floured surface. With the long side facing you, spread the butter to the edges. Fold the top third towards you to the middle, then the bottom third over this to make a smaller rectangle.

Cut into twelve 3.5 x 11 cm strips, then cut each strip lengthways down the centre, leaving attached at one end. Twist the strips around themselves 3 times to create a twisted knot, tucking the ends under the bun. Place the buns on 2 baking sheets lined with baking paper. Cover and rest in a warm place until doubled in size.

Preheat the oven to 190°C (375°F). Glaze the buns with egg wash and sprinkle with pearl sugar. Bake until golden brown.

Heat the spiced sugar and 50 ml water gently to dissolve the sugar, then boil for 3 minutes to make a syrup. Cool. Brush the buns with the syrup 2–3 times while cooling.

Bakeries

You don't have to go far early in the morning in the narrow streets of Copenhagen to experience the smell of freshly baked bread and rolls. There is a bakery on almost every corner. Recently, artisanal-style bakers have outgrown the typical chain bakeries, so now you can see young hipster bakers in beautiful open-spaces embracing heritage grains, adopting slow-fermenting, natural-starter dough and using traditional baking methods.

You'll find breads such as sourdough, formbrød and rye bread, of course, but then there are the rolls, including rundstykker, håndværker, gifler and hvedestykker – everyone has their favourite. Using traditional flavours such as cinnamon, cardamom and poppy seeds, these artisanal bakers are making sweet pastries as delicious as they are flaky.

TEBIRKES
danish poppy seed pastry

Makes 12 ▪ Preparation: 1 hour, plus 30 minutes proving ▪ Cooking: 20 minutes

Ingredients

100 g marzipan, chilled and shredded

100 g caster sugar

100 g unsalted butter, softened

1 quantity of Basic Danish Pastry Dough
   (page 26)

1 egg yolk beaten with 2 tbsp milk, to glaze

100 g (⅔ cup) poppy seeds

Beat the marzipan, sugar and butter in a food processor or stand mixer until smooth. Set aside.

Roll out the dough on a lightly floured surface to a large rectangle, about 40 x 25 cm and 3 mm thick. With the short sides of the rectangle nearest to you, spread the marzipan butter in the centre third, lengthways. Fold one-third over the filling, then brush with water. Fold the final third of pastry over the top to enclose. Cut the pastry into 5–6 cm wide pieces. Transfer to 2 baking sheets lined with baking paper and cover loosely with oiled plastic wrap. Leave in a warm place for 30 minutes, or until just under doubled in size.

Preheat the oven to 200°C (400°F). Brush the pastry with the egg wash and thickly coat with poppy seeds. Bake for 20 minutes until well-risen and golden brown. If the marzipan filling oozes out a bit, leave it to cool slightly so it can all lift up together from the baking paper. Serve warm or at room temperature.

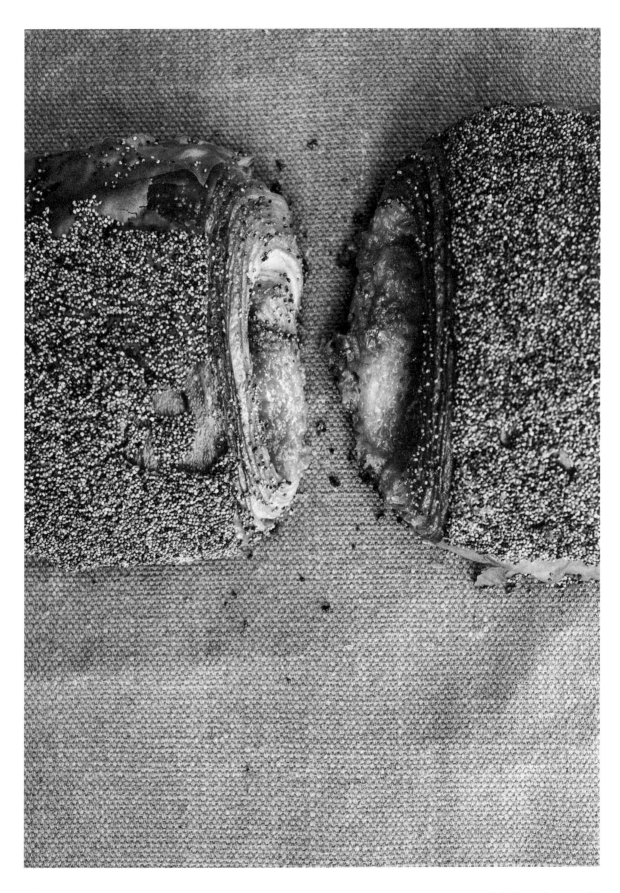

Cold Meats & Cheeses for Breakfast

In cafés, it is common to see a simple breakfast platter of a few slices of different cold meats, cheese, unpasteurised salted butter and rye or sourdough bread, which you put together and take away. It's super simple.

Røget skinke (top left): a classic smoked ham, and a perfect addition to cheese at the breakfast table. Leg or shoulder ham is available in all butchers and delicatessens.

Rullepølse (bottom right): this is pork belly that has been flattened and dry-cured in a salt rub for 24 hours, then spread with herbs or cracked black pepper and salt.

Hamburgerryg (bottom left): the pork loin is cleared of skin and fat, cured in brine for 2 days, hung for a further 3 days to dry, then smoked for several hours.

Danbo (top left, page 35): a mature semi-soft cow's milk cheese. A bacteria wash is put over the rind to prevent mould forming and helps give the cheese a slightly acidic, aromatic taste.

Vesterhavsost (top right, page 35): a Danish cheese made from cow's milk. It is has a dry texture, a strong taste and is quite salty.

Bernstein Grubé (bottom right, page 35): a cow's milk cheese that's creamy in texture and mild in flavour, with a slight saltiness.

Mycella (bottom left, page 35): a Danish blue cheese made from cow's milk. It is strong in flavour.

This is a traditional dish, particularly suitable for young children. Porridge can be served at any time of the day and with different ingredients. The basic grain is oats, but it can be flaked buckwheat, quinoa, barley, rice or rye.

GRØD
porridge

Serves 4 ▪ Preparation: 20 minutes ▪ Cooking: 30 minutes

Ingredients

BASIC PORRIDGE

120 g oat flakes, steal-cut oats, barley
 or a combination of oats and rye
1 litre (4 cups) milk (can also be a nut milk,
 such as cashew or almond)
1 tsp salt

PURÉED APPLES

500 g apples, peeled, cored and quartered
1–2 tbsp brown sugar
1 vanilla bean, split lengthways

TO ASSEMBLE

2 bananas, sliced
1–2 apples, diced
50 g toasted almonds, roughly chopped
A drizzle of honey or Caramelised Milk Sauce
 (page 40)

Mix the grains with the milk and salt in a large saucepan then gently bring to the boil, stirring. Reduce the heat very low, partially cover and cook for 20 minutes until the grains are swollen and tender but still have a little bite to them. The grød should have a thick consistency.

For the puréed apples, cut the apples into 2 cm pieces. Place in a saucepan with the sugar, vanilla bean and 4 tbsp water, cover, and cook over low heat for 20 minutes until the apples are soft and cooked down, with a few lumps. Taste the apples and adjust with sugar if needed. Scrape the vanilla seeds into the mixture. Discard the pod.

Top the grød with puréed apple, sliced banana, chopped apple and almonds and drizzle with honey or Caramelised Milk.

Toppings for Grød

*Mix and match with any of these toppings with your favourite base grød (page 38)
to create a deliciously different breakfast every morning.*

Roasted Nuts

Makes 225g ▪ Preparation: 5 minutes
▪ Cooking: 20 minutes

Ingredients
225 g almonds, cashews, hazelnuts or pistachios
½ tsp salt
1 tbsp soft brown sugar

Preheat the oven to 180°C (350°F). Rub the nuts
with the salt, sugar and 2 tbsp water. Place on a
baking tray and roast for 20 minutes.

Freeze-dried Berries

Serves 1 ▪ Preparation: none
▪ Cooking: none

Ingredients
1 tablespoon freeze-dried raspberries,
    strawberries, cherries or sea buckthorn

Add to a bowl of porridge as the finish touch to
add a touch of tartness and crunch.

Stewed Rhubarb & Yoghurt

Serves 4 ▪ Preparation: 5 minutes
▪ Cooking: 20–25 minutes

Ingredients
350 g rhubarb, chopped
75 g (⅓ cup firmly packed) soft brown sugar
50 g raspberries, strawberries or redcurrants
1 pinch of ground cinnamon or
    cardamom (optional)
1 large tbsp plain yoghurt

Place the rhubarb, sugar, 2–3 tbsp water and
berries in a saucepan and cook for 20–25 minutes.
Flavour with the spice. Spoon the yoghurt onto each
bowl of grød and top with the stewed rhubarb.

Caramelised Milk Sauce

Serves 4 ▪ Preparation: 5 minutes
▪ Cooking: 3 hours

Ingredients
240 g can condensed milk

Place the condensed milk in a large saucepan,
add enough water to cover, partially cover with
the lid and cook over low heat for 3 hours,
adding extra water if the pot is running dry.
Cool completely, then open the can and spoon
out the golden brown sauce.

Roasted Nuts

Stewed Rhubarb & Yoghurt

Freeze-dried Berries

Caramelised Milk Sauce

FRESH COD
with chickpeas

Serves 4 ▪ Preparation: 1 hour, plus 8 hours soaking ▪ Cooking: 1½ hours

Ingredients

CHICKPEAS

500 g (2½ cups) dried chickpeas, soaked in cold
  water overnight, then drained and rinsed

1 dried bay leaf

FISH BROTH

1 kg white fish bones and trimmings

½ garlic bulb

1 small onion, halved

1 tbsp fennel leaves

COD

675 g cod fillet or steaks (or other firm white fish),
  cut into large pieces

1 tbsp fine salt

1 small bunch of flat-leaf parsley

TO ASSEMBLE

4 thick slices sourdough bread, toasted

1 small handful coriander

Juice of 1 lemon

4 tbsp extra-virgin olive oil

4 soft-boiled eggs (page 24)

Place the chickpeas in a large saucepan, cover with water and bring to the boil, skimming the surface. Partially cover and simmer for 1 hour. Season and cook for a further 15 minutes until tender. Drain.

Season the cod all over with salt, cover and chill for 1 hour.

Meanwhile, for the broth, put the fish bones and trimmings into a large pot and cover with 4 litres of water. Add garlic, onion and fennel, and ring to the boil, skimming the surface. Simmer for 30 minutes until the broth is quite clear. Season. Cool slightly, then strain through muslin.

Put the cod in a large saucepan and cover with water. Add the parsley and simmer for 5–8 minutes until cooked through. Cool, then flake into large pieces.

To assemble, place the toast in a serving bowl. Heat 1 litre of the fish broth with half the chickpeas. Remove from the heat and add the fish. Season to taste with lemon juice, olive oil, salt and pepper. Stir in 1 large tbsp coriander. Ladle over the toast, top with the eggs, remaining coriander and black pepper.

SMOKEHOUSES

Smoked food holds a very important within the food culture of
Copenhagen, and Denmark as a whole. While it may have developed
as a method of preservation, it's now used largely for the unique
flavour that it lends to meat and seafood, each technique giving a
different result. This chapter introduces the wide variety of smoked
foods commonly found in Copenhagen, and shows how best to enjoy
them, either as one component of a recipe or on their own.

Sol over Gudhjem – this is the traditional name for this plate of herring and its trimmings. This dish is a classic from the small island of Bornholm, where Copenhagen locals like to go in summer. The island is known for its rocky coastline and smokehouses.

RØGET SILD
traditional smoked herring

Serves 2 ▪ Preparation: 16 minutes ▪ Cooking: none

Ingredients

2 whole smoked herrings

TRIMMINGS

2–4 thin slices rye bread

25 g salted butter

1 small red onion, thinly sliced into rings

4 radishes, shaved on a mandoline

1 egg yolk

2 tbsp snipped chives

2–4 chive flowers (optional)

Place a smoked herring on each serving plate and divide the trimmings between the plates. If chive flowers are available, tear the petals from the flowers and scatter over the plates.

To eat, lightly butter the bread, peel the skin from the smoked fish, then flake the fish, discarding the bones, and place on the bread. Layer with onion rings, radishes and spread some egg yolk on top. Sprinkle with chives and sea salt to finish.

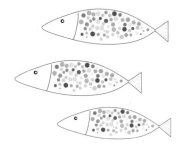

Hot-smoked salmon means that the smoking occurs with heat and the texture of the fish is very flaky. Cold-smoked salmon is actually cured by low-temperature smoking. The proteins are not cooked, hence the very fine texture of the flesh.

RØGET LAKS
smoked salmon, hot & cold

Serves 2 ▪ Preparation: 20 minutes ▪ Cooking: 30 minutes

Ingredients

100 g stale rye bread, very thinly sliced

80 ml (⅓ cup) grapeseed oil

50 g Parmesan cheese, finely grated

80 ml (⅓ cup) buttermilk

2 tbsp apple cider vinegar

1 tbsp snipped chives

1 tbsp chopped parsley

4 large organic eggs

A splash of milk

15 g salted butter

150 g hot-smoked salmon

1 large handful pea tendrils

1 handful baby English spinach leaves

1 handful watercress

150 g cold-smoked salmon

Preheat the oven to 180°C (350°F). Brush the bread with 2 tbsp of the oil and sprinkle with Parmesan. Place on a baking tray lined with baking paper. Bake for 20 minutes until crisp.

Meanwhile, make a dressing by whisking the buttermilk, vinegar and remaining oil together. Mix in the chives and parsley, then season to taste.

Beat the eggs in a bowl, add the milk and season with salt. Whisk for 1–2 minutes until frothy.

Heat the butter in a 20 cm frying pan over medium heat until frothy. Add the eggs and cook for 1–2 minutes until just starting to set. Start to draw the eggs into the centre of the pan, letting the wet mixture run out to the sides. Fold like this gently until the eggs are just set.

Flake the hot-smoked salmon into a bowl and fold in 2–3 tbsp of the dressing. Add the salad leaves and toss gently. Season to taste.

To assemble, divide the hot-smoked salmon salad between 2 serving bowls, add the cold-smoked salmon then the scrambled eggs. Finish with the rye croutons and serve with extra dressing.

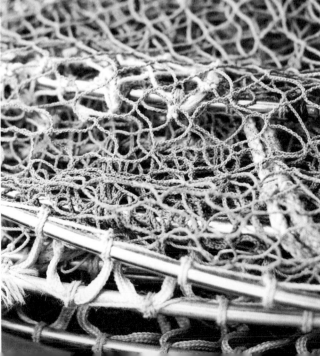

Smokehouses

Even though a lot of the large-scale smoking has moved out of the city, you can still find groups of local fishermen smoking fish on a smaller scale. It can be sometimes be hard to approach these small communities, but if you do make their acquaintance you may be able to procure a little of their delicious freshly smoked fish.

Of course, a wide variety of smoked fish are available at the fishmongers and supermarkets – smoked fish of all kinds really are an important ingredient at the lunch table.

Smoked Meat

The artisanal butchers in Copenhagen sell both fresh and cured meats and take great pride in both the husbandry of the animals and their recipes and practices for curing meats.

Bacon (left): Denmark and bacon go hand in hand. There is a wide variety available, including the very commercial type, and others that are more artisanal where the breed of pig then the practice of curing are both geared to giving a well-flavoured bacon.

There are two methods for traditional bacon – wet- or dry-cured. Wet-cured means a brine with salt and nitrite, spices, seasoning and sugar. Dry-cured means the pork is cured in a dry mixture of salt, sodium nitrate and spices. Once cured, the pork is hung to dry and mature. Both these methods result in a bacon that is lightly salty and aromatic in flavour. The bacon is then most often smoked with the rind left intact. The bacon is available to buy from the butcher, either in big slabs or thinly sliced.

Hot-smoked sausages (centre left): cured lamb, beef and pork sausages are hung in the smokehouse to take on the characteristic smoke flavour. The sausages dry and can be eaten like salami. The thin sausages are known as beer sausages (ølpolser in Danish) or snack sausages.

Venison (centre right): beechwood-smoked venison is common in Denmark. You can buy either the topside or tenderloin. It is often very thinly sliced and served as lunch on rye bread with a side of scrambled eggs, or thinly sliced as a snack with drinks.

Salami (far right): each butcher tends to have their own recipe for different types of salami, such as beef flavoured with garlic (pictured here wrapped in striped linen) or the white Pusta, which is a Hungarian beef-based salami (here wrapped in white linen). Salami is served throughout the day in Denmark, for breakfast, on sandwiches, or smørrebrød and for snacks between meals.

Everything here can be cooked in the same pan, which will incorporate the lightly smoked flavour from the bacon and sausages into the scrambled eggs. The bread can also be lightly toasted in the pan too.

COPENHAGEN BREAKFAST
smoked bacon and sausages with scrambled egg

SERVES 2 ▪ Preparation: 20 minutes ▪ Cooking: 25 minutes

Ingredients
4–6 rashers of traditional bacon, thinly sliced

10–15 smoked mini sausages

4 organic eggs

2 tbsp milk

2–4 thin slices rye bread, toasted

2 tbsp Dijon mustard, to serve

Put the bacon in a large frying pan and cook over medium heat for 5–8 minutes on each side until it starts to sizzle. Move to one side of the pan, add the sausages and cook, turning occasionally, for 5–8 minutes until they start to colour. Remove from pan, reserving 2 tbsp bacon fat in the pan.

Beat the eggs, milk and salt and black pepper together. Return pan to medium heat, and when the fat is sizzling, add the eggs and cook for 1–2 minutes until beginning to set. Start to draw the egg into the centre, allowing the wet egg to run to the sides, then continue to draw the eggs in and fold them over each other for a further 3–5 minutes until just set. Serve with the bacon and sausages, toast and Dijon mustard.

Smoked Fish

The Danish name for a smokehouse is a røgeri. These smokehouses were originally attached to fishing villages, very close to the fishmerman's cottages, and can be recognised by their distinctive chimneys.

You will find many of these traditional smokehouses in Bornholm (the local summer retreat for some Copenhagen locals) where the fish is delicately smoked over the smouldering embers of the fire. Smaller smokehouses have now become established in Copenhagen itself where local fishermen smoke fish for family and friends. Smoked fish are served with raw onion rings, herbs, such as chives or dill, pickles of all kinds and rye bread or crackers (knækbrød).

Cold-smoked salmon (top left): each smokehouse has their own way of smoking salmon; some like to cold-smoke salmon hanging, whiles others lay them down. Salmon that is smoked flat is quite oily and is typically served sliced very thinly.

Whitefish (bottom right): cold-smoked in the same way as salmon, whitefish is usually more heavily salted than other smoked fish, and is often served with scrambled eggs and fresh herbs, such as parsley.

Hot-smoked ocean trout (bottom left) & salmon: these can be smoked whole or in fillets. The flesh is very flaky.

Smoked eel (far right): the flavour is sweet and delicate, but also rich due to its high fat content. Spread on crackers or rye bread.

Smoked herring (second from right): raw herring are smoked either by being hung from large hooks in the smoker or else butterflied, boned and placed flat on a grill. The flavour is relatively soft and mild compared with other smoked fish. Use in omelettes and salads.

Smoked mackerel (third from right): unsmoked mackerel is naturally strong in flavour, and smoking adds even more character. It is smoked in the same way as herring, and the process turns the skin a stunning gold and dark grey-black colour.

Smoked plaice (top): also known as bakskuld, and similar to flounder, this fish is cleaned and smoked whole. It can be eaten as is, or fried. Serve with rye bread, butter, sliced red onions and pickles.

*Rygeost is the Danish version of ricotta.
It's a little firmer in texture, with a light
sour taste and a characteristic smoked
flavour. It's also easy to make at home.
Serve it with salad, herbs and crusty bread
or crackers at brunch or lunch.*

RYGEOST
hay-smoked cheese

Serves 4 ▪ Preparation: 15 minutes, plus 2 hours draining ▪ Cooking: 10 minutes, plus 2 minutes smoking

Ingredients

2 litres organic whole milk

200 ml organic buttermilk

1 tsp sea salt, plus extra to serve

3–5 drops rennet

1 tsp caraway seeds

TO SMOKE THE CHEESE

1 large handful of hay/oat straw or rye straw,
   and damp green nettles (optional)

Heat the milk, buttermilk and salt in a large saucepan to 26°C (79°F). Add the rennet and leave for 1 hour until the mixture is set into large curd.

Place the curd in a sieve lined with muslin and drain for 1 hour. Discard the watery whey.

Line a perforated dish, about 10 cm diameter and 5 cm deep, with muslin. Taste the curds and season with a little more salt, if needed. Spoon into the container and leave over a bowl to drain for 1 hour.

To smoke, wet the hay, place in the bottom of a lidded saucepan and add the nettles, if using. Place a wire rack over the top. Remove the cheese from the muslin and place on the rack. Place the saucepan over medium–high heat, once you see smoke come through, cover with the lid and smoke for 30–60 seconds. Turn the cheese over, cover and smoke for another 30 seconds.

Season with caraway seeds and sea salt and serve with crackers and vegetables.

LUNCH

Lunch can often be thought of as something to be eaten on the run, but just as much effort goes into preparing and enjoying this meal as any other. Smørrebrød can be eaten many ways: as takeaway, at a counter or in a restaurant. But in all cases each ingredient in these elaborate open sandwiches are one carefully chosen to complement each other. Herring and snaps also feature strongly in Copenhagen's lunch repertoire, as do sausages and burgers.

Herring

Denmark has more than 7000 km of shoreline, which goes some way to explaining its love of seafood, and herring in particular. The appreciation of herring dates back to Viking times, when the fish was preserved in salt; in the Middle Ages herring began to be preserved in vinegar.

Preserving herring

There are a variety of tradtional methods of preserving herring, no doubt dating back to an time when refrigeration was not as sophisticated as it is today.

First, fresh herring are gutted and packed whole in salt for as long as a year. At this stage you can buy them in large cans packed tightly with salt.

To use salt-packed herring, the head, tail and skin first need to be removed. The fillets are then soaked in water for up to 48 hours to remove the saltiness. Pre-soaked herring fillets can be found in fishmongers, and it's these soaked fillets that are used to prepare pickled (white) or marinated (red) herring.

Pickled or marinated herring can be served at any occasion, from everyday meals to celebrations, although the variety of accompaniments for the herring depends on the occasion. On special occasions, for example, the pickled herring are arranged on a large platter and served with boiled, chopped or sliced eggs, capers, chopped red or white onions, mayonnaise or sour cream mixed with dill, crème fraîche and lightly toasted rye bread.

This chapter has some of the most classic preparations for preserved herring, as well as a recipe for fresh filleted herring cooked and served in a brine (page 72).

Homemade pickled white herring are used in open sandwiches. The basic spices are coriander, mustard seeds and cloves, but family recipes vary. More spices and other flavourings such as cinnamon, allspice, bay leaves and citrus peel may also be added.

PICKLED WHITE HERRING

Makes 12 ▪ Preparation: 30 minutes, plus 6½ hours soaking & 3 days curing ▪ Cooking: 30 minutes

Ingredients

8 salted herring fillets, soaked in
   cold water for up to 6 hours, drained,
   and refrigerated until needed
2 tsp coriander seeds
2 tsp allspice
2 tsp mustard seeds
1 tsp cloves
2 tsp black peppercorns

1 cinnamon stick, halved
150 ml apple cider vinegar
150 ml dry sherry or white wine
75 g (⅓ cup) sugar
2 dried bay leaves
2 strips lemon zest
1 onion, sliced into rounds

Place herring in a bowl, cover with water and leave for 30 minutes. Rinse and pat dry on paper towels.

Meanwhile, add all the spices to a deep, dry frying pan and toast for 2–3 minutes. Add the vinegar, sherry, sugar, bay leaves, lemon zest and 150 ml water. Swirl the pan to dissolve the sugar, then heat until the liquid just comes to the boil. Simmer for 20 minutes, then leave until cold.

Cut the herring fillets into 5 cm-wide pieces. Place the sliced onion in layers in between the slices of fish in a glass or ceramic jar, then pour over the cold brine. Seal and chill for 3 days before serving. Keep for up to 1 month in the fridge.

These herring can be used straight from the cure, or serve as the base for different recipes, such curried herring (page 70). You need to use the natural red food colouring sandalwood and the preservatives salt petre and citric acid to give the fish their red colour and flavour.

MARINATED RED HERRING

Makes 1 kg (about 12 servings) ▪ Preparation: 45 minutes, plus 6 hours soaking & 2 weeks marinating ▪ Cooking: none

Ingredients

1 kg salted herrings fillets, soaked for
   6 hours or overnight
1 tsp whole allspice
½ tsp red sandalwood (buy online)
1 tsp whole cloves
1 tsp ground ginger
7 g Spanish hops

2 dried bay leaves
1 tsp salt petre powder (buy online)
1 tsp citric acid
250 g muscovado sugar
125 g coarse sea salt
375 ml (2½ cups)vinegar

Pat the herring dry on paper towels. Put the allspice, sandalwood, cloves, ginger, hops, bay, salt petre and citric acid in a mortar and lightly crush with the pestle. Mix with the sugar and salt – this is the 'cure'.

Cut the fish into 5 cm-wide pieces. Sprinkle some of the cure on the base of a large resealable glass or ceramic jar and place a layer of fish on top. Continue layering. Mix the vinegar with 125 ml (½ cup) water and pour over the fish until completely covered. You may need to add a little extra water. Seal, and allow to chill for 2 weeks. Store for up to 1 month. Serve with mayonnaise, krydderfedt (bacon or pork dripping), capers, sliced red onions, dill and rye bread.

The Danes have integrated spices such as cinnamon, cloves, black pepper and curry into their cuisine, especially with flavouring and preserving their beloved herring. This particular recipe is from Lise Rudolph, Christine's grandmother.

KARRYSILD
curried herring

Serves 4 ▪ Preparation: 10 minutes ▪ Cooking: none

Ingredients

2 heaped tbsp mayonnaise

100 ml crème fraîche or sour cream

2 tsp Madras curry powder

225 g Red Marinated Herring (page 69),
   plus 1–2 tbsp pickling liquid

Mustard, cress, soft-boiled eggs (page 22)
   and sliced red onion, to serve

Mix the mayonnaise and crème fraîche together in a small bowl. Add the curry powder and pickling liquid from the red herring. Taste and adjust the seasoning with salt and black pepper or a little more curry powder, if liked. Fold in the herring.

To assemble, spread thinly sliced rye bread with krydderfedt (bacon or pork dripping), then top with the curried herring and a little mustard and cress. Serve with boiled eggs and sliced red onion.

This herring dish is served chilled for lunch as a topping for rye bread. Add some of the pickled red onions and extra dill or parsley, if liked. This recipe was given to us by our friend Samina Langholz, which she adapted from her grandmother.

FRIED HERRING
in vinegar

Serves 4 ■ Preparation: 45 minutes ■ Cooking: 30 minutes

Ingredients

BRINE

200 g brown sugar

2 dried bay leaves

10 black peppercorns

5 white peppercorns

1 tbsp chilli flakes (optional)

1 red onion, thinly sliced

400 ml white vinegar (distilled,
   or apple cider vinegar)

HERRING

8 fresh herring, boned and butterflied
   (about 1.5 kg cleaned weight)

2 tbsp Dijon mustard

2 tbsp coarsely chopped dill

2 tbsp coarsely chopped flat-leaf parsley

50 g rye flour

50 g unsalted butter

2 bronze fennel sprigs, to garnish

Put the sugar, bay, peppercorns, chilli and 200 ml water, in a deep saucepan and heat to dissolve the sugar, stirring well. Bring to the boil, then simmer for 20 minutes. During the final 5 minutes, add the sliced red onion. Remove from the heat and add the vinegar. Cool.

Season the herring, spread the flesh with a little of the mustard and sprinkle with a little dill and parsley, then fold the halves together. Put the flour on a shallow plate, season with salt and mix with a fork.

Coat the fish all over with the seasoned flour, shaking off any excess.

Melt the butter in a large non-stick frying pan over medium–high heat, add the fish, pressing down well with the spatula, and cook for 4 minutes on each side until crisp and browned on the outside. Drain on paper towels and place in a large shallow dish. Pour the pickling vinegar over the fish and leave to cool to room temperature. Cover and chill for up to 12 hours before serving. Garnish with fennel sprigs.

Smørrebrød

To have a proper lunch in Copenhagen, it has to include smørrebrød. Considered the national dish of Denmark and loved by many people across the world, there are many opinions about how to create the perfect smørrebrød – this bread (99 per cent will be rye bread), that grain, butter or mayo, fish fried or sautéed, eggs sliced or quartered, the list is endless. From lunchboxes to fancy restaurants, they are found everywhere. Even if it's the smallest gathering for lunch at home, you will be provided with a variety of toppings and bread options.

Old & New Smørrebrød

Recently, the trend towards smørrebrød – the open sandwich – for lunch has been revitalised. This is credited to young chefs with the New Nordic Food mentality, where each layer of the open-sandwich complements the other. Here are two versions: a classic, and a more modern take.

Modern Smørrebrød (top)

BREAD: small piece of rye bread or sourdough, or a white bread made from heritage grains

SPREAD: with crème fraîche, horseradish cream or lemon mayonnaise

SEAFOOD: cured or smoked salmon

SOFT-BOILED EGG: cut into quarters, the yolk is still very golden and almost jammy in texture

SALAD: simple shaved fennel in lemon juice, or sauerkraut made from a vegetable other than cabbage – possibly fennel, cucumber or leafy greens such as chard

EXTRA: the fashionable crisp rye bread

GARNISHED: with flat-leaf parsley, microgreens such as red or green basil, shiso leaves, mustard cress or radish sprouts

Traditional Smørrebrød (bottom)

TOASTED BREAD: rye or rustic white bread. Not always small, half a slice or a whole one

SALAD: a frilly green lettuce leaf, sometimes there may be some cucumber or tomato

HARD-BOILED EGG: where the yolk is very well done and the egg is most often sliced with an egg slicer

SPREAD: mayonnaise or sour cream

SEAFOOD: cooked prawns

GARNISHED: with a twist of lemon, cucumber and nearly always dill

This traditional recipe for plaice (in two styles) on toasted bread has been served at Restaurant Schonnerman for many years. Locals and tourists have been enjoying lunches at this restaurant since 1877.

STJERNESKUD
plaice, fried & steamed

Serves 1 ▪ Preparation: 30 minutes ▪ Cooking: 10 minutes

Ingredients

THOUSAND ISLAND DRESSING

60 ml (¼ cup) mayonnaise

2 tsp tomato ketchup

60 ml (¼ cup) dry white wine

½ tsp paprika

1 tsp Worcestershire sauce

CRISPY PLAICE

2 plaice (or flounder) fillets, about 75g each

1 tbsp plain flour

1 egg, beaten

20 g (⅓ cup) panko breadcrumbs

Oil, for deep-frying

STEAMED PLAICE

75 ml dry white wine

1 plaice (or flounder) fillet, about 100g

TO ASSEMBLE

1 slice of white bread, toasted

1 tsp butter

60 g (¼ cup) mayonnaise

8–10 small cooked prawns, peeled

1 tbsp black caviar (or other fish roe)

1 dill sprig

Lime wedges, to serve

Mix all the dressing ingredients together and season to taste.

For the fried plaice, season the fish, then dip in the flour, shaking off excess, then dip in the beaten egg and finally the panko breadcrumbs. Heat enough oil for deep-frying in a deep saucepan to 170°C (340°F). Deep-fry the fish for 3–4 minutes until golden brown and cooked through. Drain on paper towels.

At the same time, steam the third fillet of fish by heating the wine in a small, deep pot until simmering. Season the plaice and fold in half. Gently place in the pot, cover, and cook for 3 minutes until opaque. Set aside.

To assemble the open sandwich, butter the toast, add a layer of dressing and put on a serving plate. Top with the steamed plaice, then the 2 crispy plaice, half on the plate, half on the toast. Top with the mayonnaise and prawns, then spoon the caviar along one side. Season, add the dill and serve with lime wedges.

SMØRREBRØD

KOLDT & LUNT ~ den "lille" FROKOST...

HAUSER PLADS 16-18 ❋ KØBE...
☎ +45 33 12 07 85 🖥 www.danskfro...
ÅBNINGSTIDER: MANDAG ~ LØRDAG 1...
FROKOST SERVERES: 11:30 - 14:00, 13.00 – 17:00 eller
LUKKET SØN- OG HELLIGDAGE
Sidste bestilling 15:30, køkken åbent til 16:00

A true rejemad uses the seasonal tiny shrimp called Fjordrejer. Because the Danes like to eat this all year round, however, the recipe is adapted where necessary. This recipe is a modern classice served by the chefs at Palægade.

REJEMAD
open shrimp sandwich

Makes 2 ■ Preparation: 30 minutes ■ Cooking: 5 minutes

Ingredients

300 g raw school prawns

1 tbsp salt

Juice of 1 lemon

2 slices of wholewheat bread, toasted

1 handful of nasturtium leaves

A few dill sprigs

LEMON MAYONNAISE

2 egg yolks

1 tsp Dijon mustard

1 garlic clove, grated on a microplane

125 ml (½ cup) neutral oil such as sunflower oil

2 tbsp lemon juice

For the mayonnaise, place the egg yolks, mustard, garlic, a pinch of salt and the oil in a tall, slim container. Starting at the bottom and working upwards very slowly, blend with a stick blender until thick. Taste for salt. Add the lemon juice and whizz until very thick. Transfer to a piping bag.

To cook the shrimp, bring a large saucepan of water to the boil. Add the salt and lemon juice, then add the shrimp and cook for 3–4 minutes until bright pink. Drain and place in a bowl of ice-cold water. Peel the shrimp, then season with salt and pepper and lemon juice, if liked.

Set the toast on serving plates. Pile the shrimp onto the toast, then pipe the lemon mayonnaise in several places. Add the herbs and sprinkle with cracked black pepper and sea salt.

Restaurant Øl & Brød by Mikkeller head chef Ben Coughlan combines traditional Danish beef tartare and an egg yolk on rye bread for a modern take on smørresbrød. He finishes it with beer-battered onion rings. Perfect.

BEEF TARTARE
with fried onion rings

Makes 2 ■ Preparation: 30 minutes ■ Cooking: 10 minutes

Ingredients

150 g beef rump, trimmed and
   cut into small dice
1 tbsp wholegrain mustard
100 g mayonnaise
2 egg yolks
2 slices of wholegrain bread
50 g Pickled Beetroot (page 100)
12 wood sorrel sprigs (or microherbs)

ONION RINGS
200 ml dark beer
50 g (⅓ cup) plain flour, plus extra
   for dusting
1 white onion, cut into 2cm slices
Oil, for deep-frying

Season the beef with salt, pepper, mustard and a drizzle of olive oil. Rest for 10 minutes, then taste and adjust the seasoning, if necessary. Mix the mayonnaise with lots of pepper, then place in a piping bag.

For the onion rings, pour the beer into a bowl, then add the flour a little at a time until thick. Dust the onion rings with flour. Preheat enough oil for deep-frying in a large, deep saucepan to 180°C (350°F). Dip the onion rings into the batter and then carefully add to the oil and cook until light golden brown on both sides. Remove, drain and season with salt.

To assemble, top each piece of bread with beef tartare, add an egg yolk in the centre, then randomly pipe or spoon the mayonnaise on top. Add the Pickled Beetroot, then add 2–3 fried onion rings on each and season. Garnish with wood sorrel.

The Danes are more than happy to take the time to peel the tiny Fjordrejer shrimp – that's how much they savour the taste – but they can also be eaten with their shells on. School prawns can too, and make a fine substitute. Serve on pancakes or open sandwiches.

PANCAKES
with shrimp

Serves 4 ◾ Preparation: 30 minutes, plus 30 minutes standing ◾ Cooking: 30 minutes

Ingredients

PANCAKES

125 g plain flour, sifted

1 good pinch of sea salt flakes

2 eggs, beaten

300 ml milk

20 g melted butter, plus extra for cooking

FILLING

50 g unsalted butter

350 g raw school prawns, shell on

1 pinch of sea salt

2 tbsp snipped chives, plus extra to garnish

250 ml (1 cup) crème fraîche

Mix the flour and salt together in a bowl. Make a well in the centre, add the eggs and milk and mix until smooth. Leave for at least 30 minutes. Just before ready to cook, stir the melted butter into the batter.

Brush a hot 20 cm non-stick crêpe pan with a little butter. Pour in 75 ml batter, swivel the pan to spread the batter and cook for 2 minutes until the surface looks set and the base is golden brown. Flip over and cook for another 1–2 minutes. Remove and keep warm. Repeat to make 8 pancakes.

For the filling, melt the butter in a sauté pan, add the prawns and cook over high heat for 3 minutes until they start to turn pink. Sprinkle over the salt and season with black pepper. Once prawns start to turn crisp remove from the heat and sprinkle over the chives.

To serve, spread 1–2 pancakes with crème fraîche. Spoon over the shrimp and sprinkle with extra chives.

The Danes like to eat seasonally, and one of the best times to see this is in late winter to early spring, when lumpfish roe is in season. Restaurants will feature lots of specials using lumpfish roe, such as simple buckwheat blini, crème fraîche and lumpfish roe platters.

LUMPFISH ROE
with crackers

Serves 2 ■ Preparation: 10 minutes ■ Cooking: none

Ingredients

100 g prepared lumpfish roe or
    150 g roe sack (ask your fishmonger)
100 ml crème fraîche
75 g finely chopped red onion
50 g salted capers, soaked in water
    for 10 minutes and drained
½–1 tsp sea salt
2 large Knækbrød (crackers; page 20)

If the roe is not cleaned, place it in a bowl and cover with water, then gently pull the fine skin away from the small roe and discard. Refresh the water, then with a small balloon whisk, whoosh the mixture a little. The whisk will catch any excess skin you may have missed. Drain and whoosh once more with cold water. Drain and pat dry with paper towels. Season with sea salt, tasting as you add the salt. Serve all the ingredients separately with large knækbrød (crackers).

Herbs

Herbs come and go into and out of fashion, and Copenhagen chefs are the first to both embrace traditional flavours, and add a new twist to give an ingredient new meaning. Herbs are not used just for presentation, but as a garnish that adds a new layer of flavour to finish a dish off.

BRONZE FENNEL: the fronds of the bronze fennel are perfect for fish, egg or chicken dishes. They are slightly tougher than conventional fennel fronds.

DILL: fresh dill is used in many dishes. The sweet celery-ish taste is excellent with fish, shellfish, eggs, chicken, tomatoes and cucumbers.

DILL FLOWERS: when the dill flower has yellow pollen, this should be used in for cooking and salad. Either place whole flowers inside fish to be grilled, or sprinkle the pollen over fish fillets as a garnish. Dill flowers that have gone into seed should be used for to make pickles and other preserves.

TARRAGON: a sweet, delicate, almost liquorice flavour. Excellent with fish, eggs and chicken and a good partner to fresh peas and broad beans.

LOVAGE: a common herb used in Denmark, similar to celery. Use with vegetables, eggs and fish.

CORNFLOWERS: a mild spicy clove flavour, which is good in salads. Simply remove the petals from the flower and sprinkle over a salad. They are also beautiful dried and sprinkled on sweet dishes.

BROCCOLI FLOWERS: these have the earthy taste of broccoli, so use in a mixed salad.

CHIVES & CHIVE FLOWERS: these are picked as soon as they have a slight woody-citrus taste. They can also be pan-fried with butter and spooned over fish or pasta.

PINE SHOOTS: green stems with purple flowers. Pull the petals from the flower and scatter over the finished dish or salad.

SWEET CECILY: also known as Spanish chervil, this herb belongs to the celery family. It's a sweet,

anise-flavoured herb with fern-like leaves that's good in fish and chicken dishes as well as in sweet dishes such as ice creams. Used to flavour aquavit and snaps too.

LEMON VERBENA: a sweet-scented green leaf, excellent used as a tea, to flavour ice cream, cakes, jam or even to flavour whipped cream to serve with fruit.

ROSEHIP PETALS: these can be freeze-dried and used to decorate desserts, or can be crushed with sugar and used to flavour sugar for baking.

ROSEHIP: this is the pod and seeds of a rose. They are similar looking to crab apples and belong to the same family as apples. Rosehip jam (page 154) is very fragrant with good body; it's a long process but worth the time and effort. Rosehip jelly is easier, but you still need to leave the mixture to strain slowly.

Sea herbs: foraging on the beach

SALAD LEAVES AND HERBS: ones that grow on the beach are characterised by their salty taste and often hardier texture. These leaves may need soaking before using and then pan-frying in a light oil or butter. If using in a salad, mix only the odd leaf in the mixture of wild forest or wood leaves.

SEA BUCKTHORN BERRIES: also known as hipster berries in Copenhagen, these are bright orange berries with a very tart taste, which are excellent freeze-dried and crumbled or made into a preserve. The leaves are great as a tea, where it acts as a brilliant antioxidant.

SEA BEANS: these beans, which look like a very young green twig with tiny offshoots, should ideally be blanched in boiling water for 30 seconds, then drained and refreshed to remove some of the salty, briny taste. Pan-fry with butter and serve with fish or chicken.

SEA KALE: this has the basic flavour of kale, but requires blanching. Shred and cook with oil and garlic.

Pea Shoots

Nasturtium

Red Wood Sorrel

Sea Kale

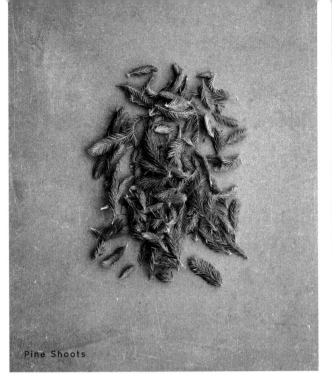

Pine Shoots

Fresh Cornflowers

Tarragon

Chamomile & Apple
Sorbet, served with
Green Strawberries & Wood
Sorrel (from Winterspring Co...)

Thomas Laursen from Wildfooding, leading forager for top restaurants in Copenhagen, has only one rule to making a good salad — keep sea herbs and leaves separate from the forest forages. Sea herbs are strong in flavour and texture and can overwhelm gentle forest leaves.

WILD LEAF & HERB SALAD

Serves 4 ■ Preparation: 10–15 minutes ■ Cooking: none

Ingredients

350 g mixed salad leaves, such as watercress or nasturtium leaves, Spanish chervil, lambs quarters or chickweed (both similar to baby spinach), pea and broad bean leaves, wood sorrel or sorrel and bronze fennel

50 g mixed flowers, if available, such as chive, nasturtium, rocket, pea and marigold (or just one kind is good too)

75ml extra-virgin olive oil, grapeseed or sunflower oil

Juice of 1 lemon, to taste

CHIVE OIL (OPTIONAL)

400 g chives, cut into smaller pieces

400 ml neutral oil

If making the chive oil, blend the chives with the oil in a blender at full speed for 10 minutes, or until it reaches a temperature of 70°C (158°F). Strain into a bowl. It is almost impossible to make smaller amounts and achieve a good result. Instead, make a big batch and freeze the rest for another day.

Place the salad leaves in a bowl of ice-cold water and whoosh around with your hands. Soak for 5–10 minutes. Drain on paper towels, then spin very gently in a salad spinner. If you don't want to dress the salad immediately, place the leaves in a resealable bag or plastic bag and chill for 12–24 hours.

To dress, place the prepared leaves and flowers in a bowl and drizzle over a little olive oil, chive oil or oil of your choice. Drizzle over lemon juice to taste and toss gently. Season at the last minute.

White asparagus is very seasonal in Denmark.
This interpretation from Admiralgrad 26 is
served raw, coated with a crust of flaxseeds
and almonds, served with a buttercream
sauce and finished with wild herbs.

WHITE ASPARAGUS
with almonds

Serves 4 ■ Preparation: 20 minutes ■ Cooking: 20 minutes

Ingredients

12 white asparagus spears

100 ml neutral oil, plus extra for brushing

25 g flaxseeds

175 g raw almonds with skins

50 g mix of wild herbs, such as wood sorrel,
　Spanish chervil and tarragon

BUTTERCREAM

150 ml double cream

100 ml buttermilk

1 ice cube

Finely grated zest of ½ lemon

Trim the woody asparagus bases with a vegetable peeler. Place the peelings in a small saucepan, add enough oil to cover and heat gently until the oil just bubbles. Cool completely. Strain the oil and set aside, discarding the peelings.

Preheat the oven to 180°C (350°F). Toast the flaxseeds and almonds in the oven for 10 minutes. Cool completely, then blitz to a coarse powder.

To make the buttercream, warm the creams in a small saucepan, then remove from the heat and stir in the ice cube. Add the lemon rind and season with salt. Cool.

To assemble, brush the asparagus spears with the oil and roll them in the flaxseed powder. Cut the asparagus into 5cm pieces on the diagonal. Place 2 spoonfuls of the cream on each plate and top with the asparagus. Garnish with the herbs.

Spices — sweet & savoury

The Danes were great travellers and adventurous explorers bringing back spices and traditions from overseas, which is seen in many of their traditional recipes where they have flavoured and brought life to basic, home-grown ingredients.

Sweet Spices

CINNAMON STICKS: this sweet bark is used in baking, but also in pickles, preserves and braises.

NUTMEG AND MACE: the lacy outer shell on nutmeg is actually mace. Both provide an earthy sweet flavour to savoury and sweet sauces, preserves and breads.

CLOVES: used for preserves and pickling.

CARAWAY: used in breads, preserves and pickles, especially pickled cucumbers. Used to flavour the traditional Rygeost cheese.

STAR ANISE: more commonly associated with Southeast Asian cooking, star anise is an almost sweet spice similar in taste to aniseed or liquorice. Use in preserve-making or with duck or red cabbage.

POPPY SEEDS: these have a nutty taste, and are sometimes reminiscent of almonds, making them perfect to use with the marzipan.

VANILLA PODS: vanilla is traditionally added to sweet dishes, but it is also a good addition to braises, adding an uplifting sweet flavour.

DRIED CORNFLOWERS: wild flowers are found all over Denmark. These are dried and used as decorations in desserts. They have a mild clove flavour.

Savoury Spices

CORIANDER SEEDS: used whole in pickling and with preserved meats, and ground to use with pork.

CUMIN SEEDS: the seeds are used to flavour herring.

BLACK PEPPERCORNS: used to flavour savoury dishes of all kinds, and now fashionably used with certain berries and dessert dishes.

BAY LEAVES: the use of bay leaves imparts a fragrant flavour to food. It is used fresh or dried to flavour stews, braises and roasts. Also used in preserved foods.

CARDAMOM: an Indian and Southeast Asian spice used to give a strong sweet, pungent flavour to food. It lends itself both to sweet and savoury dishes. Excellent with ham, braises and perfect for spiced biscuits and bread-based bakes too.

CURRY POWDER: the curry mix in Denmark is very light in flavour and not hot at all. It is more fragrant than anything else. It is mixed with a creamy base such as sour cream and/or mayonnaise to create a light spicy sauce for herring, eggs and meats.

JUNIPER BERRIES: these provide that 'pine-like' flavour, and are excellent with game and preserved meats, or in braises and stews.

ALLSPICE: interesting how one spice can taste like a mixture of cloves, cinnamon and nutmeg. Used in pickling, sausage making, as well as in slow-cooked dishes.

DILL SEED: used in pickles and preserves.

DILL FLOWERS GOING INTO SEED: used in pickling.

The Horseradish

Fresh horseradish can be grated, ground or chopped. It releases an astringent taste and aroma that opens up your nasal passages and tingles your nose. It can be harsh if not eaten in moderation or initially with care.

Cream Sauce with Horseradish

Makes 130 ml ▪ Preparation: 5 minutes

Ingredients

100 ml crème fraîche or whipped cream
1 pinch of salt
2 tbsp finely grated horseradish
1 dash of malt vinegar

Mix the crème fraîche, salt, horseradish and vinegar together in a bowl.

....

Horseradish Cream

Makes 350 ml ▪ Preparation: 5 minutes

Ingredients

200 ml cream
1½ freshly juiced horseradish
1 tbsp apple cider vinegar
1 pinch of salt
100 g horseradish, grated on a microplane

Lightly whip the cream, then add the horseradish juice and vinegar and season with the salt. Transfer to a bowl and cover with the grated horseradish. (Recipe from Mia Christiansen, Barr restaurant.)

Salsa Verde

Makes 300 ml ▪ Preparation: 5 minutes

Ingredients

15 g flat-leaf parsley, coarsely chopped
15 tarragon leaves
1 tbsp thyme leaves
1 French shallot, coarsely chopped
2 tbsp sherry vinegar
250 ml extra-virgin olive oil or grapeseed oil
75 g horseradish, grated

Using a food processor or blender, blitz the herbs, shallot, vinegar, oil and grated horseradish until smooth.

....

Buttermilk Dressing

Makes 150 ml ▪ Preparation: 5 minutes

Ingredients

100 ml buttermilk
2 tbsp finely grated horseradish
1 tbsp snipped chives
2 tsp red wine vinegar
1 pinch of sugar or drizzle of honey

Mix the buttermilk, grated horseradish, chives, and vinegar together and season. Taste and adjust with the sugar or honey to balance out the taste of sweet, salty and hot.

Pickles

A variety of pickles are served with an assortment of dishes served in Denmark, and none more than for a smørrebrød spread. The style can be a quick pickle, which is ready within 30 minutes, short-term pickles to be cured for 5 days, or long-term pickles.

Quick Red Onion Pickles

Makes 500 ml ▪ Preparation: 20 minutes, plus 30 minutes standing ▪ Cooking: 5 minutes

Ingredients

350 g red onions, thinly sliced

2 tbsp salt

125 ml (½ cup) distilled white vinegar
  or apple cider vinegar

1 tsp sugar

2 tbsp spices (peppercorns, coriander
  seeds or mustard seeds, or a mixture)

Place the onions in a colander and sprinkle with 1 tbsp of the salt. Leave for 10 minutes. Meanwhile, heat the vinegar with the remaining salt, the sugar and spices. Once the salt and sugar have dissolved, remove from the heat and add 250 ml (1 cup) cold water. Wash the salted onions and pat dry. Add the onions to a bowl and cover with the brine. Leave for at least 30 minutes. Drain.

24-hour Beetroot Pickles

Makes 500 ml ▪ Preparation: 20 minutes, plus 24 hours chilling ▪ Cooking: 20 minutes

Ingredients

500 g beetroot

250 ml (1 cup) distilled white vinegar
  or apple cider vinegar

2 tbsp salt

3 tbsp sugar

2–3 tbsp mixed spice

Cook the beetroot in a pan of boiling salted water for 20 minutes until just al dente. Mix the vinegar with the salt and sugar and heat until the salt and sugar dissolve. Add the mixed spice and cool, then mix with 250 ml (1 cup) cold water. Peel the beetroot and slice into 0.5 cm slices or into wedges 1 cm thick. Place the beetroot in a jar and pour over the pickling mix. Chill for 24 hours. Store for up to 5 days before serving.

Long-term Pickles

Makes 500 ml ▪ Preparation: 20 minutes, plus 24 hours chilling ▪ Cooking: 5 minutes

Ingredients

350–500 g choice of vegetables

1 quantity of brine (see above)

Slice or cut your choice of vegetables: beetroot about 1 cm thick; cauliflower into florets; pickling cucumbers left whole or halved lengthways; carrots halved lengthways. Fit tightly into sterilised jars. Follow the instructions for the twenty-four hour brine, then pour the hot brine into the jars. Seal. Leave for 1 month and store for 3–6 months.

The Pariser bof is a traditional lunchtime or dinner dish that has made a comeback in restaurants all over Copenhagen. It is 100 per cent good-quality beef, pan-fried and served on toast with pickled beetroot, horseradish, onions, capers, a pickle and a raw egg yolk.

PARISERBØF
old-fashioned burger

Serves 4 ▪ Preparation: 25 minutes ▪ Cooking: 5 minutes

Ingredients

500 g good-quality beef, minced
50 g unsalted butter

ACCOMPANIMENTS
4 thin slices rye bread, lightly toasted
50 g coarsely grated horseradish
1 onion, finely chopped

75 g salted capers, soaked for 10 minutes
  and drained
150 g Pickled Beetroot (page 100), drained
150 g piccalilli
4 organic egg yolks
1 handful of salad leaves, such as nasturtiums,
  rocket or baby spinach

Put the minced beef into a bowl and season. Divide into 4 portions and roughly shape into patties.

Melt the butter in a large frying pan, add the beef patties and cook for 1–2 minutes each side, keeping the meat rare inside.

Serve each patty on a slice of toast with a small amount of each of the accompaniments.

GASOLINE BURGER

This burger joint opened in 2016 and has been hailed as one of the best burgers in the world. It's a kiosk at a disused gas station in the city and part of its philosophy is to close when the last burger is sold. Serve with fries seasoned with herb oil and a sauce.

Gasoline Burger

Serves 4 ∎ Preparation: 30 minutes
∎ Cooking: 5 minutes

Ingredients

600 g grass-fed chuck minced beef

4 slices of Cheddar cheese

4 potato or brioche buns

1 red onion, sliced into rings

150 g sour-sweet pickled cucumbers

8 tbsp Thousand Island-style sauce

Preheat a grill pan or cast-iron frying pan. Season the meat and roughly shape into 4 patties. Brush the patties with a little oil and sear for 1–2 minutes on each side until well browned, but still very juicy. Sit the cheese on the hot burger.

Toast the buns in the grill pan.

To build, place the base of the bun on a serving plate, top with the patty and melted cheese, then the onion, pickles and sauce. Sandwich with the top bun. Serve.

Thousand Island-style Sauce

Ingredients

2 egg yolks

1 tsp Dijon mustard

1 tbsp white wine vinegar

300 ml grapeseed oil

1 tsp tomato purée

1 tsp Worcersthire sauce

1–2 tbsp crème fraîche

1 splash of Tabasco

For the sauce, whisk the egg yolks, mustard and vinegar together in a bowl, then, whisking constantly, gradually add oil in a steady stream until a thick consistency is reached. Mix in the remaining ingredients and season.

Seasonal Summer Herb Oil

Ingredients

25 g chervil, coarsely chopped

25 g tarragon, coarsel chopped

25 g flat-leaf parsley, coarsely chopped

1 garlic clove, coarsely chopped

250 ml whipped cream

50–100 ml neutral oil

For the oil to serve with the fries, blitz the herbs, garlic and cream in a blender. Add oil to barely cover and blend, adding more oil until you reach the desired consistency. Season with pepper.

Fries

For crinkle-cut fries, serve with toppings of your choice. In the summer it's a fresh herb dip. Offer salt, vinegar and truffle salt as well as the usual sauces and dips.

L | EXTRAS

ORGANIC FRIES	KR 25,00

TOPPINGS FOR FRIES

VINEGAR SALT	KR 5,00
TRUFFLE SALT	KR 5,00
HERB OIL	KR 10,00

HOMEMADE DIPS	KR 10,00

MAYO, CHILI MAYO
GASOLINE SAUCE,
SEASONAL (ASK)

EXTRAS FOR BURGERS

ADD CHEESE	KR 10,00
ADD DOUBLE MEAT	KR 30,00

DESSERT	KR 35,00

LEMON MOUSSE
CHOCOLATE MOUSSE

COMBOS

GASOLINE COMBO	KR 110,00
BURGER, FRIES, SODA	
FULL COMBO	KR 135,00
BURGER, FRIES, SODA, DESSERT	
DOUBLE TROUBLE COMBO	KR 325,00
2×BURGERS, 2×FRIES, 6-PACK TUBORG RÅ	
+ 2×DESSERT	+ 45,00
+ BEER OR LEMONADE	+ KR 10,00
+ JARRITOS	+ KR 20,00

DRINKS

SODAS	KR 25,00
COCA COLA, COCA COLA ZERO,	
SQUASH, RAMLØSA	
ORGANIC HOMEMADE LEMONADE	KR 35,00
JARRITOS	KR 40,00
TUBORG RÅ (ONLY TAKE-AWAY)	KR 30,00
6-PACK	KR 150,00

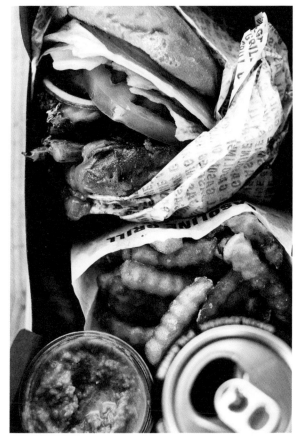

K UP HERE

den økologiske pølsemand

HAY

THE DANISH
KEJSER SAUSAGE

SOULLAND

Hot Dogs

The tradition of hot dog stands and carts has been embraced by modern 'foodsters' all over Copenhagen, bringing the quality and variety of sausage and hot dogs, add-ons and breads to a new level. It's all about choice. There is now the organic hot dog, which has more meat and is served on wholegrain bread. Hot dogs are the first kind of fast food to find its way to Denmark.

The hot dog carts are known as pølsevogn. Pølse is the word for sausage/hot dog. The sausages are boiled and/ or grilled, but can be just served boiled; it's your choice.

Hot dogs are often eaten by the stands. They are wrapped in butcher's paper, but eating without making a mess is still a challenge – but don't worry, that's part of the fun.

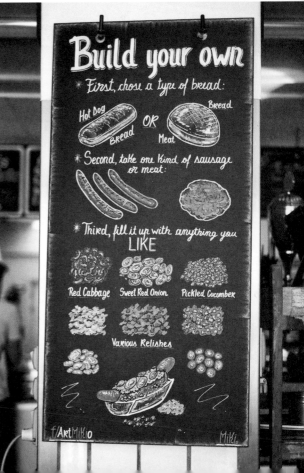

The classic Copenhagen hot dog is either a boiled or a grilled wiener sausage with a line on each side of ketchup, remoulade, mustard and fresh onion, all topped with cucumber pickle.

HOT DOG
lamb or pork sausage buns

Serves 4 ▪ Preparation: 10 minutes ▪ Cooking: 20 minutes

Ingredients

8 good-quality sausages

4 long white buns

1 tbsp each of 4 different toppings
   of choice (page 110)

Preheat the oven to 200°C (400°F). Place the sausages on a baking tray and roast for 20 minutes, or until cooked through. Alternatively, grill the sausages for 6–12 minutes, or until cooked through.

Cut the buns in half through the middle, but not all the way through, and toast. Put a sausage in the middle, then add your choice of topping. A Fransk is a traditional way of serving a long grilled pork sausage in a hollowed out French baguette with a similar choice of toppings.

The types of sausage to choose from include:

All-pork hotdogs:
these can be smoked with beechwood, and might include spices such as cardamom and nutmeg

All-beef sausages:
an alternative to the classic pork sausage

Bratwurst:
known as the medisterpølse, this sausage is flavoured with cloves and allspice

Hot Dog Toppings

To dress a hot dog the traditional Copenhagen way you will need a combination of sour, spicy, sweet and greasy toppings.

Onion Marmalade

Makes 250 g ■ Preparation: 15 minutes
■ Cooking: 45 minutes

Ingredients

2 tbsp neutral oil
25 g unsalted butter
500 g onions, thickly sliced
1 dried bay leaf
1 tsp lightly crushed black peppercorns
1 tsp sea salt flakes
2 tbsp sugar

Heat the oil and butter in a pan. Stir in the onions, then add the bay leaf, peppercorns, sea salt and sugar. Cook very slowly for about 45 minutes, stirring frequently until the onions are very tender, browned and shiny in colour. The juices, if any should be very syrupy. Taste and adjust seasoning, if necessary, with salt.

Simple Remoulade

Makes 150 ml ■ Preparation: 5 minutes

Ingredients

150 ml mayonnaise
1 tbsp wholegrain mustard
1 tbsp chopped capers
1 tsp traditional Indian curry powder
1 tsp chopped black peppercorns

Mix all the ingredients together. Season with salt if necessary.

Quick Crunchy Pickles

Makes 350 g ■ Preparation: 10 minutes, plus 30 minutes standing ■ Cooking: none

Ingredients

1 cucumber, chopped, or 225 g sliced
   red cabbage
2 tbsp fine salt
50 g fine sugar
100 ml distilled white vinegar
1 tsp black peppercorns, lightly crushed

Place the cucumber in a colander set over a bowl and sprinkle with the salt. Leave for 10 minutes, allowing the juices to drip into the bowl. Squeeze the cucumber with your hands to rid of any excess juices, then place in a bowl, add the sugar, vinegar, peppercorns and 100 ml cold water. Soak for 20 minutes before serving.

Apple Ketchup

Serves 1 ■ Preparation: 5 minutes

Ingredients

2½ tbsp tomato ketchup
1 tsp spiced apple sauce

Mix together and serve.

DRINKS

Denmark is well known for its internationally acclaimed beers
Carlsberg and Tuborg, but there is much more than this. Copenhagen
offers a myriad of micro-breweries with eclectic flavours; it is a
leading city when it comes to natural wines, and the level of schnapps
and aquavit on offer is mind-blowing. This chapter takes us through
these three main groups of drinks – snaps, wine (and what to do with
the leftovers: make vinegar of course) and beer, with a classic recipe
of pork cheeks with beer. Skål!

Craft Beers

The most famous large breweries in Denmark are Carlsberg and Tuborg who brew traditional beers on a large scale. Micro-brewing, however, has become very popular in the last 12 to 15 years, and many craft beer enthusiasts brewing different types of beer on a small scale have sprung up all over Denmark, including Mikkeller and Friends. The beautifully designed microbrewery establishments have ten to 40 beers on offer at any one time and have become trendy places to eat and drink in as the brewers have started to collaborate with top Danish chefs.

Every part of the pig is used in Danish cooking and it's common to see pork cheeks for sale. This traditional recipe of braising pork cheeks in beer with celeriac, carrots and onion, is given its modern look with how it is served.

PORK CHEEKS
slow cooked in beer

Serves 4 ▪ Preparation: 30 minutes ▪ Cooking: 2–2½ hours

Ingredients

12 pork cheeks, about 675 g total

3 tbsp chopped thyme leaves

25 g salted butter

2 tbsp extra-virgin olive oil, plus
    extra for drizzling

175 g celeriac, finely diced

100 g carrots, finely chopped

1 small onion, finely chopped

500 ml (2 cups) dark beer

Mashed celeriac or potato, to serve

CHARRED ONIONS

1 of each small–medium red, white and yellow
    onions, peeled and kept whole

1 tbsp honey

2 tbsp thyme leaves

Preheat the oven to 180°C (350°F). Pat the pork cheeks dry. Mix the thyme with salt and pepper and use to season the meat. Reserve any thyme seasoning.

Melt the butter in a 7.5 cm-deep ovenproof frying pan. When sizzling, add the pork and brown for 8 minutes on each side. Set aside on paper towels.

Add a little oil to the pan, then add the vegetables. Sauté for 10 minutes until just starting to brown. Gradually add the beer, scraping the base of the pan. Once bubbling, return the pork to the pan, adding more water to make sure it's submerged. Bring to the boil, cover with wet baking paper, then cover with the lid and braise in the oven for 1½–2 hours.

Once the pork cheeks are tender, remove and keep warm. Boil the juices and vegetables in the pan on top of the stove until the juices are thick. Taste, adding some of the thyme seasoning.

For the onions, cook them in a pan of boiling water for 8 minutes. Drain, then cut lengthways through the middle. Heat a large frying pan over high heat, add the onions, cut-side down, and cook until they brown and char. Drizzle over a little oil and flip the onions over. Drizzle over some honey and season with salt and pepper and thyme. Cook for 2 minutes until charred in places.

Serve the pork with the sauce, onions and mashed celeriac or potatoes.

Snacks for Drinks

There are a variety of different salts to be found in the Copenhagen salt repertoire – sea salt has gone a long way with its flavourings. Liquorice salt is quite common, as is seaweed salt, and both complement fresh vegetables and nuts very well.

Radishes with Salt

Serves 4 ▪ Preparation: 5 minutes

Ingredients
2 handfuls of radishes
Butter, to serve

Serve the radishes sprinkled with sea salt flakes with butter on the side.

Peas with Horseradish

Serves 4 ▪ Preparation: 5 minutes

Ingredients
1–2 handfuls of raw pea pods
Pea flowers and horseradish, to serve

Place the pea pods in a bowl, sprinkle with a little fine sea salt, fresh pea flowers and freshly grated horseradish and serve.

Kohlrabi with Liquorice Salt

Serves 4 ▪ Preparation: 5 minutes

Ingredients
1 kohlrabi, peeled, cut in half and
   cut into 4mm thick slices

Serve the kohlrabi sprinkled with liquorice salt or put the salt in a bowl and dip the the kohlrabi into it.

Roasted Almonds with Seaweed Salt

Serves 4 ▪ Preparation: 5 minutes

Ingredients
225 g almonds
1 tbsp extra-virgin olive oil
1–2 tsp seaweed salt

Preheat the oven to 180°C (350°F). Rub the almonds with the oil. Place on a baking tray and toss with the seaweed salt. Roast for 20 minutes. Cool before serving.

Radishes

Peas

Kohlrabi

Roasted almonds

Fresh berries, such as red- or blackcurrants, raspberries, blackberries, strawberries or gooseberries can be used to make fruit schnapps. Try adding a vanilla pod to the mixture, spices, such as cardamom or star anise, or herbs, such as mint or thyme.

SNAPS
schnapps

Makes 1 litre ■ Preparation: 15 minutes, plus 1 week macerating time ■ Cooking: none

Ingredients

1 kg redcurrants, raspberries or berries
  of your choice, wiped clean and dried
1 vanilla pod, split lengthways
750 ml unflavoured schnapps or vodka
  (40% alcohol content, 80 proof)

Place the berries and vanilla pod in a 1 litre jar with a tight-fitting lid, then top with the alcohol. Cover and leave in a cool dark place (about 20°C/68°F) for at least a week, or until the berries have sunk to the bottom. At this point the schnapps can be served. However, if left for longer, the flavour will be mellower than just a sharp fruity taste. You can leave the fruit for up to 3 months before serving. Shake the bottle and taste it occasionally to check on it.

Flavourings

The common herbs, often from the wild, used in making schnapps are myrtle, blackthorn, beach wormwood, woodruff, juniper, yellow bedstraw, pine shoots (tips) and Spanish chervil.

Sabotøren

Håndværksvine til Værtshuspriser

Her kan man drikke vin i glas eller direkte fra flasken!

Der er også lidt at spise, hvis man da ikke tager vinen med hjem

tirs-tors fre-søn [søndag 12]
16-24 13-24

— HVAD MED NOGET MILJØ-HALLO!!?

Natural Wine

Natural wines begin with how the vines are grown. In Denmark they need to be ecologically certified. You will probably have noticed that more wine menus now include orange or skin-contact wines, but the sheer number of natural wines can make it confusing to understand exactly what it is. Skin-contact wines are white wines produced like red wines, using natural fermenting methods. Nothing extra is added to start the fermenting process. Grapes are mashed, put into a barrel or container and placed in a controlled environment. The colour the wine takes on depends on the amount of time the skins are left in the grape mixture. It could be hours or weeks. If hours, the wine is lightly tinged with orange, but if left longer the colour becomes more vibrant. These wines have the characteristics of red wine, such as a fuller body and more tannin yet they maintain the acidity of white wine, so can stand up to red meat.

When it comes to cooking in Copenhagen, the majority of restaurants don't like to waste anything. Leftover wines, beers, ales or lagers can be fermented to make natural vinegars.

VINEGARS
homemade

Makes 400ml ■ Preparation: 10 minutes, plus 3–4 weeks fermenting ■ Cooking: none

Ingredients

RED, WHITE OR FORTIFIED WINES
100 ml unfiltered vinegar
200 ml wine
100 ml water

BEERS, ALES OR LAGER
100 ml unfiltered vinegar
300 ml beer, ale or lager

Mix the vinegar with the wine and water or the beer and place in a clean bottle or wide-lipped jar. Cover with muslin and secure with string or a rubber band. Keep the jar or bottle in a dark place at room temperature.

After a few days a 'film' will start to form. If you can see a colour (it might be greyish) this is the 'mother' developing. Store for a few more weeks, then taste. If it has a sweet mellow taste and isn't too sharp then start to use it. It can take up to 2 months.

Strain the finished vinegar through an unbleached coffee filter into clean bottles and secure with lids. As it's unpasteurised, store in the fridge.

IN-BETWEEN

An afternoon break is considered a necessity among Copenhagen locals. This will most likely involve a snack of some kind, either something sweet, such as ice cream, or something savoury, such as a herb dip with vegetables. It's all part of the relaxed culture enjoyed in Copenhagen. Benches and seating are scattered all over the city for everyone to take a break along the harbour, quays or parks. During winter, cafés offer a cosy atmosphere with fireplaces to sit by and relax with friends over coffee and a snack.

The traditional apple cake in Copenhagen is a triple-layered concoction of apple sauce, almond macaroon crumble and spiced whipped cream. It is usually finished with a spoonful of redcurrant jelly, but here rosehip jam is served for its fragrant floral quality.

ÆBLEKAGE
apple cake with macaroons & cream

Serves 6 ▪ Preparation: 1 hour ▪ Cooking: 25 minutes

Ingredients

100 g marzipan or almond paste, grated

¼ teaspoon each of ground cardamom and cinnamon

60 g icing (confectioners') sugar, sifted, plus 1 tbsp

1 egg white

1 kg fragrant apples, peeled and diced

Finely grated zest of 1 lemon, plus 2 tbsp lemon juice

50 g unsalted butter

100 g golden caster sugar

3 lemon verbena sprigs or 1 tsp ground cinnamon

200 ml double cream

100 g crème fraîche

Preheat the oven to 150°C (300°F). Put the marzipan in a bowl and beat in the spices with an electric whisk. Gradually add the 60 g icing sugar, alternating with the egg white until a batter is formed. Place heaped tablespoons of batter on 2 baking trays lined with baking paper, spacing them well apart. Bake for 20–25 minutes until puffed and golden brown. Leave for 10 minutes, then cool on a wire rack.

Meanwhile, mix the diced apples with the lemon zest and juice. Melt the butter in a frying pan, add the apples and mix to coat with butter. Add the caster sugar and cook, stirring, until the sugar dissolves. Add the lemon verbena and cook until the apples are tender, but not mushy. Cool. Discard the verbena.

Put the cream in a bowl and sift in the 1 tbsp extra icing sugar. Add the crème fraîche and whisk gently to mix, then more vigorously until thick. Divide the apple sauce among 6 bowls, crumble up 2 macaroons per bowl, then top with 2 heaped tbsp of the cream mix. Serve with Rosehip Preserve (page 154), if liked.

This recipe, adapted from chef and cookbook author Mikkel Karstad's beautifully delicious cookbook Gone Fishing, *usually calls for apples, but feel free to change the fruit according to the seasons — we opted for rhubarb.*

RABARBERKAGE
rhubarb and marzipan cake

Serves 10 ▪ Preparation: 30 minutes ▪ Cooking: 40–50 minutes

Ingredients

500 g rhubarb, sliced into 5cm long pieces,
  about 2.5mm thin

1 tsp ground cinnamon

1 tbsp Demerara sugar

150 g unsalted butter, softened

150 g (⅔ cup) soft brown sugar

150 g marzipan, chopped

4 eggs (about 150g)

5 tbsp plain flour

Finely grated zest of 1 lemon

Crème fraîche, to serve

Preheat the oven to 170°C (340°F). In a bowl, toss the sliced rhubarb with the cinnamon and sugar, then leave for at least 20 minutes.

Meanwhile, mix the butter, sugar and marzipan in a food processor until smooth. Gradually add the eggs, then the flour and lemon rind. Spread the batter into an oiled 20cm cake tin lined with baking paper and top with rhubarb. Bake for 40–50 minutes until set and the fruit is caramelised. If the fruit is browning too much, cover with foil and cook the cake until set in the centre. Cool for 1 hour.

Serve warm or at room temperature with crème fraîche.

HINDBÆRSNITTER
raspberry bars

Makes 12 ▪ Preparation: 45 minutes, plus 30 minutes chilling ▪ Cooking: 20–25 minutes

Ingredients

375 g (2½ cups) plain flour

75 g almond meal

200 g sugar

1 vanilla bean, split lengthways
   and seeds scraped out

275 g chilled unsalted butter,
   cut into cubes

1 egg, beaten

500 g (2½ cups) raspberry jam

1 egg yolk beaten with 2 tbsp milk,
   to glaze

50 g (¼ cup) demerara sugar

Process the flour, almond meal, sugar and vanilla seeds in a food processor to mix well. Add the butter and process until it resembles fine breadcrumbs. Gradually add the egg and pulse until the mixture comes together as a dough. Divide into 2 equal pieces. Shape each into a disc about 3 cm thick. Cover and chill for 30 minutes.

Place each piece of dough between 2 sheets of baking paper and roll out to 3 mm thick. Chill for 30 minutes, still in the paper.

Preheat the oven to 190°C (375°F). Remove the dough from the paper and place on a clean surface. Prick each piece all over with a fork. Place one piece of dough on a baking tray lined with baking paper and spread the jam on top, leaving a 2cm border. Place the second piece of dough on top. Press from the middle to remove air. Prick with a fork. Brush the surface with egg glaze and sprinkle with Demerara sugar. Bake for 20–25 minutes until golden brown. Cool briefly, then cut into bars while still slightly warm. Cool completely on a wire rack. Serve.

Liquorice

Liquorice is a root with a strong aniseed flavour. It is sourced from Calabria in southern Italy, as well as from Southeast Asia, Iran and Afghanistan. Thanks to the use of liquorice as an ingredient in top-end Copenhagen restaurants, it's more than a sweet, it's a staple spice.

Vast amounts of liquorice are consumed in Denmark, where it is made into a salty liquorice confectionery, a powder, granules or an extract to add to ice creams and caramels, or transformed into salt to be sprinkled on savoury dishes. It's also excellent with berry jam and tastes good with dark chocolate and game meats.

Liquorice bark or stick: this is excellent in cooking. Bruise it, then steep it in hot liquids such as milk or water as a basis for custards, sauces, syrups or tea. You can also add it to sugar to make liquorice sugar or use it in brines and salt cures to flavour meat and fish.

Powdered liquorice: this can be added straight to dishes. It's good to experiment because the flavour can be quite strong. You'll find Danish companies producing liquorice powders from different countries, such as Italy and Asia – all with different levels of sweetness and saltiness.

Liquorice granules: these granules are 100 per cent liquorice extract and will dissolve in liquids when heated. They can also be eaten as they are, but the flavour is very intense and a little bitter.

Liquorice salt: liquorice root is mixed directly into salt flakes. The flavour is intense. Team with earthy-flavoured vegetables, such as caiuliflower, kohlrabi and kale.

Liquorice slab: this is made by mixing liquorice root extract with sugar, water and gelatine to make a thick malleable paste. Melt to use for caramels or syrups.

Snacks

Copenhagen locals like to have a small break during the day, so eating a snack is the perfect excuse. There are many ways of taking a break in Copenhagen. Sit on a doorstep or on one of the many benches along the harbour and enjoy an ice cream while watching the world go by. Visit one of the contemporary afternoon teahouses and order a fancy cake. Or, buy some of the flavoured caramels or beetroot-powdered flødeboller and eat them while a strolling along one of the narrow streets. You can also stop in one of the trendy wine bars for a late afternoon wine.

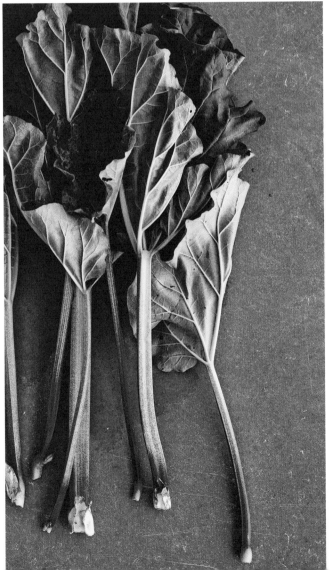

KARAMELLER
homemade caramels

Makes 48 ▪ Preparation: 15 minutes, plus 30 minutes standing ▪ Cooking: 45 minutes, plus 8 hours cooling

Ingredients

180 ml (¾ cup) double cream

1 vanilla bean or ½ tsp vanilla bean paste,

   or ½ tsp sea salt flakes (such as fleur de sel),

   or 1 liquorice stick or 1 tsp liquorice granules

160 g golden or corn syrup

225 g granulated sugar

60 g salted butter, cubed

Freeze-dried berries (optional), to garnish

Heat the cream in a saucepan to just below boiling point, then remove from the heat and add your chosen flavour. Leave for at least 30 minutes to infuse.

Meanwhile, in a deep, heavy-based saucepan, add the syrup and sugar and heat gently for the sugar to dissolve completely. Bring to the boil and bubble until the syrup reaches 115°C (239°F). Remove from the heat and add the cream, it will bubble. Stir well to mix and return to the heat. Leave it to bubble until the mixture reaches 127°C (261°F).

Remove the pan from the heat and stir in the butter until smooth. Pour into a 20 cm square tin lined with foil and brushed with oil. Sprinkle with extra salt or freeze-dried berries, if liked. Cool on a wire rack for 4–6 hours or overnight.

Remove from the tin, then the foil and cut the caramels into 2.5 x 1 cm rectangles. Wrap in baking paper. Store in the fridge.

FLØDEBOLLER
chocolate-coated meringues

Makes 20 ■ Preparation: 1 hour, plus cooling & setting ■ Cooking: 30 minutes

Ingredients

300 g marzipan

300 g caster sugar

¾ tsp natural edible beetroot powder
   (buy online)

5 egg whites (150g)

1 tsp cream of tartar

400 g white chocolate, chopped

Preheat the oven to 180°C (350°F). Roll out the marzipan to about 5 mm thick and cut out 20 discs about 4 cm in diameter. Place on 2 baking trays lined with baking paper and bake for 7 minutes. Cool.

Meanwhile, dissolve the sugar in 100ml water over low heat. Add ¼ tsp beetroot powder, swirl the pan to combine, then bring to the boil and boil for 2 minutes until a light syrup. Whisk the egg whites with the cream of tartar in a standmixer until doubled in size. Add the syrup in a slow steady stream, whisking on high. Once all the syrup is added whisk for 10 minutes until glossy and very stiff. Transfer to a piping bag fitted with a 1 cm plain nozzle and pipe onto the marzipan discs. Chill.

Place 300 g of the chocolate in a heatproof bowl set over a pan of barely simmering water and stir until melted. Very finely chop the remaining chocolate. The melted chocolate should be 45–50°C (113–122°F). Remove a third of the melted chocolate and leave in a warm place. Place the finely chopped chocolate into the remaining two-thirds chocolate and stir to melt. It should go down to 26–27°C (79–81°F). If there is any unmelted chocolate remove it. Add the reserved melted chocolate and stir to bring it to 28°C (82°F).

To coat the flødeboller, first dip the base, then place on baking paper and chill to set, then dip the top into the melted chocolate to coat. Dry on a wire rack until cool. Dust with the remaining beetroot powder.

This is a buttermilk and yoghurt summer dessert served throughout Denmark. The buttermilk and yoghurt sauce is served with ginger biscuits and strawberries. Here, Chef Ben Coughlan from Øl & Brød in Copenhagen shares his recipe.

KOLDSKÅL
summer buttermilk soup

Serves 6 ▪ Preparation: 1 hour, plus chilling ▪ Cooking: 20 minutes

Ingredients

KOLDSKÅL

2 egg yolks

2 tbsp caster sugar

520 g (2 cups) natural yoghurt

500 ml (2 cups) buttermilk

Finely grated zest of 1 lemon,
  plus 2 tbsp lemon juice

1 vanilla bean, split, seeds scraped

TO ASSEMBLE

600 g strawberries, hulled and quartered

200 g mini ginger biscuits

A few wood sorrel leaves (optional), to serve

For the koldskål, whisk the eggs and sugar together until light and fluffy, then gradually start to add the yoghurt followed by the buttermilk, lemon zest and juice and vanilla seeds. Taste and adjust the level of lemon juice and sugar, if necessary. Chill well before serving.

To assemble, randomly arrange the strawberries and biscuits in 6 bowls and add a few wood sorrel leaves to each bowl. Pour the buttermilk sauce into the bowl at the table. Serve.

The flavour of the ice cream is up to you.
Make the most of what's in season with herbs,
spices, flowers and fruit, such as raspberries,
gooseberries, rose petals, chamomile flowers,
lemon verbena, mint or even liquorice bark.

ICE CREAM

Makes 600ml ▪ Preparation: 25 minutes, plus 1 hour steeping ▪ Cooking: 15 minutes, plus 2 hours cooling, chilling & churning

Ingredients

250 ml full-cream (whole) milk

150 g granulated sugar

A good pinch of salt

5 egg yolks

375 ml (1½ cups) double cream

Heat the milk, sugar and salt in a saucepan, stirring to dissolve the sugar. Don't boil the milk. Beat the egg yolks, then whisk the milk into the eggs in a steady stream. Return to the pan and heat gently, stirring until the custard just thickens and coats the back of the spoon. Pour into the cream and stir to mix. Cool to room temperature, then chill for at least 30 minutes. Churn in an ice cream maker according to manufacturer's instructions.

To add flavour, heat the cream and add either the scraped seeds of 1 vanilla bean, 1 piece of liquorice bark, 1 tbsp cloves, 1 broken cinnamon stick, 1 tbsp bruised cardamom pods, 2 sprigs of lemon verbena, a handful of camomile flowers or 4 tbsp instant coffee granules. Steep for 1 hour. Strain, then continue as above.

If using berries, crush 225 g berries with a fork and add 100 g sugar, depending on the ripeness. Let the sugar dissolve and stir through the base. Alternatively, spoon the churned ice cream and berry purée into a container and freeze.

MINI TOP

VANILLA

CHOCOLATE

30

45

45

CARD
ONLY

POPSICLE
blackcurrant

Makes 12 ■ Preparation: 45 minutes, plus 4–8 hours freezing ■ Cooking: 15 minutes

Ingredients

350 g blackcurrants

100 g caster sugar, plus 2 tbsp extra

3 egg yolks

300 ml double cream, lightly whisked

1 tsp vanilla bean paste

200 g white chocolate, broken into pieces

50 g freeze-dried blackcurrants (buy online),
   lightly crushed

Heat the blackcurrants and the 2 tbsp sugar gently in a saucepan until the sugar dissolves and the currants swell and burst. Cook for 3–5 minutes until the blackcurrants are roughly puréed. Cool completely.

Put the remaining sugar in another saucepan and add 125 ml (½ cup) water. Cook slowly to dissolve the sugar. Bring to the boil, then simmer for 5 minutes until the syrup thickens. A sugar thermometer should read 108°C (226°F).

Put the egg yolks in a heatproof bowl. Using a stick blender, whisk the eggs, slowly pouring in the hot syrup in a steady stream. The mixture should become lighter in colour and very thick. Fold in the cream, vanilla and blackcurrant purée. Pour into 12 popsicle moulds and insert a stick. Freeze for 4–8 hours.

Melt the chocolate, place in a measuring jug and cool slightly. As soon as you pop the popsicle from the mould, gently push it into the melted chocolate and lift up, leaving a 2cm border at the base. Lay on baking paper and sprinkle freeze-dried blackcurrants on one side. Freeze again until needed.

Emil Eshardt-Nielsen, chef at the dessert bar WinterSpring, shares this recipe for a delicate, seasonal tart, which is a perfect snack for that when you are not quite hungry, but need something in between meals.

PEA TART
with smoked cheese

Makes 6 tarts ▪ Preparation: 45 minutes, plus 14 hours chilling ▪ Cooking: 30 minutes

Ingredients

250 g (1⅔ cups) wholemeal flour

10 g sugar

5 g salt

150 g unsalted butter, diced
   and chilled

1 egg

FILLING

6 eggs

100 g smoked soft cheese,
   such as rygeost (or gouda)

50 g salted butter

150 g fresh podded peas

A few drops of lemon juice

3 tbsp neutral oil

50 g pea tendrils and flowers

Blitz the flour, sugar and salt in a food processor to combine. Add the butter and pulse until the mixture resembles fine breadcrumbs. Whisk the egg with 15 ml water, then gradually add to the flour, pulsing until it comes together as a dough. Chill for 14 hours.

Divide the dough into 6, then roll out each piece to fit 6 x 10cm greased fluted tart tins. Pierce the bases with a fork and trim excess. Chill for 30 minutes.

Preheat the oven to 160°C (325°F). Line the pastry with baking paper and dried beans. Bake blind for 10 minutes, then remove the beans and baking paper and bake for 10 minutes until the pastry is crisp and golden.

Now, make the filling. Whisk eggs and cheese together. Season with salt and pepper. Divide among tarts and bake for 8–10 minutes until just set to the touch, but still wobbly. Cool for 5 minutes.

Put the butter into a heatproof bowl set over a pan of simmering water. As the butter starts to melt, whisk with 2 tablespoons water, this mixture will stay in a runny emulsion. Add the peas and fold together. Season to taste and add 1–2 drops of lemon juice. Spoon over the tarts.

Place the tarts on plates. Whisk the remaining lemon juice with the oil to make a vinaigrette. Season. Add the pea tendrils and toss to coat. Place over the tarts and sprinkle with pea flowers.

There's a remoulade to suit every occasion. The base is a creamy sauce (mayonnaise, crème fraîche, yoghurt or skyr), which is then mixed with pickled vegetables and fresh herbs. Serve with seasonal vegetables for a healthy snack between meals or with drinks.

CREAM & HERB DIP
with vegetables

Serves 4 ▪ Preparation: 20 minutes ▪ Cooking: none

Ingredients

200 ml crème fraîche

100 ml skyr (or thick Greek-style yoghurt)

Finely grated zest and juice of ½ lemon

1 tbsp Dijon mustard

4 tbsp finely chopped capers

4 tbsp finely chopped gherkins

1 small onion, finely grated

8 radishes, finely chopped

50 g mixed chopped herbs, such as dill, flat-leaf parsley and tarragon

5 tbsp whipping cream, lightly whipped

500 g mixed baby carrots, sliced cucumbers and radishes, to serve

Mix the crème fraîche, skyr, lemon zest and juice and mustard until smooth. Stir in the capers, gherkins, onion, radishes and herbs. Taste and season with salt and pepper. Gently fold in the whipped cream. Serve with baby carrots, cucumbers and radishes.

Preserves are served throughout the meal in Copenhagen. Rosehips should be picked in autumn, and gooseberries are available in early summer. Jytte Rudolph, Christine's mother, kindly passed these recipes to us.

PRESERVES
seasonal harvest

Gooseberry Jam

Makes: 5 x 225 g jars ▪ Preparation: 30 minutes ▪ Cooking: 25-30 minutes

Ingredients
1 kg gooseberries
900 g granulated sugar

FLAVOURS
elderflower blossoms; 1 tbsp cardamom pods, lightly crushed; 2 cinnamon sticks; 3 lemon verbena sprigs; 3 rosemary sprigs; or 3 large lemon thyme sprigs

Place the gooseberries and 300 ml water in a large saucepan and add the elderflower blossom, tied in muslin, if using. Cook gently for 15 minutes until the berries have softened.

Add the flavouring of choice, or if using elderflowers, remove and squeeze the muslin into the pot. Stir in the sugar until dissolved. Increase the heat and boil for 10 minutes, stirring. Check for setting: place a spoonful of jam on a cold plate, chill for 5 minutes, then if the jam wrinkles, setting point is reached.

Pour into sterilised jars, cool, cover and chill, or cover immediately and boil in a canning pot for 15 minutes to vacuum seal. If canning, the preserve will be good for up to a year if unopened.

Rosehip Preserve

Makes 6 x 225 g jars ▪ Preparation: 2 hours ▪ Cooking: 1¼ hours

Ingredients
1 kg rosehip berries
50 ml cider vinegar or lemon juice
300 ml rosewater (made by pouring boiling water over collected rose petals and infusing for 2 days) or water
1 vanilla bean, seeds scraped out

Remove the top and bottom (stem and blossom end) of each rosehip, and slice on down side to open. Scoop out the centre and discard.

Place the rosehips in a large pot with vinegar and 200 ml water. Bring to the boil, then simmer for 15-20 minutes until the rosehips are almost tender. Add the rosewater, sugar and vanilla seeds and cook, stirring to dissolve the sugar. Cook for 10-15 minutes, then check for setting (see left).

Pour the jam into clean jars, then cool, cover and chill, or cover immediately and boil in a canning pot for 15 minutes to vacuum seal. If canning, the the preserve will be good for up to a year unopened.

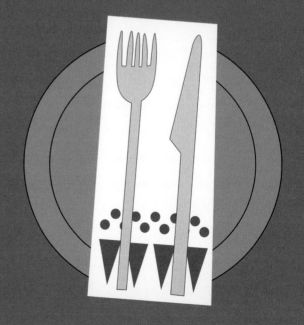

DINNER

The people of Copenhagen like to dine out, but they also welcome the opportunity to entertain and eat at home with family and friends. Rich traditional stews, soup and roasts are all part of 'come in from the cold' winter meals. Then with the slightest of sunshine Copenhagen locals love nothing more than an outside barbecue — they open out their tables in the courtyards and light the grill for social gatherings.

COD TARTARE
with asparagus

Serves 4 ▪ Preparation: 20 minutes, plus 4 hours standing ▪ Cooking: 10 minutes

Ingredients

300 g sashimi-grade skinless cod fillet
  (or other sashimi-grade white fish)
50 g rye bread, sliced
1–2 tbsp extra-virgin olive oil
8 thick asparagus spears, shaved into long
  lengths with a vegetable peeler
50 g red mizuna or other mustard leaves
2–4 tbsp pickled mustard seeds (see tip)

MUSTARD MAYONNAISE
2 egg yolks
1 tsp wine vinegar
2 tsp Dijon mustard
200 ml rapeseed oil

Season the cod with salt and leave for at least 4 hours in the fridge.

Meanwhile, preheat the oven to 140°C (275°F). Dry the bread in the oven for 10 minutes until crisp. Cool, then blitz in a food processor until fine crumbs form.

Mince the cod using 2 knives, cutting in opposite directions. Season with the olive oil and extra salt if needed.

For the mayonnaise, mix the egg yolks, vinegar and mustard in a blender. Gradually pour in the rapeseed oil while the machine is running. Transfer to a piping bag or bowl.

Divide the fish among 4 serving plates. Add the asparagus and mizuna, then add 3–4 small dabs of mayonnaise on each plate and some pickled mustard seeds. Sprinkle with the bread and finish with herb flowers and/or dill.

Tip: for pickled mustard seeds, boil 50 g yellow mustard seeds in water about 9 times, draining and using clean water each time. Mix 300 ml apple cider vinegar, 300 ml water and 300 g sugar together in a saucepan and heat to dissolve the sugar. Add the mustard seeds and bring to the boil. Cook for 10 minutes, then cool. Makes 600ml

A frikadelle is a meatball made with minced pork and veal, but it can be made with fish as well. In Copenhagen the meat mixture can be bought already minced together, so you just need to add your own spices and flavourings.

FRIKADELLER
meatballs

Serves 4 ▪ Preparation: 15 minutes ▪ Cooking: 8–12 minutes

Ingredients

300 g minced pork

300 g minced veal

2 tbsp plain flour

1 tsp juniper berries, crushed

1 onion, finely grated

1 egg

50 g butter, for cooking

Chopped flat-leaf parsley, to serve

With your hands, mix the minced pork and veal with salt, pepper and flour, then add the juniper berries and grated onion. To taste for seasoning, fry a tiny amount in a small amount of butter. Adjust seasoning if required. Beat the egg, add to the meat mixture and mix well to combine.

Melt the butter in a frying pan over medium heat. Dip a large oval spoon in the butter, then use to take a scoop of the meat mixture. Using the palm of your hand, shape into an oval. Add to the frying pan. Continue to shape the meat mixture to make 12 ovals in total.

Cook for 8–12 minutes, turning several times until golden brown and cooked through. You can finish in a hot oven to make sure the meatballs are cooked through. Serve with Boiled Potatoes with Lovage (page 188), Pickled Cucumbers (page 100) and chopped parsley.

Skipperlabskovs, which translates as 'the captain's stew', is a beef and potato stew traditionally cooked for sailors while out at sea. The beef was cured with salt then stewed slowly with potatoes. This recipe was given to us by chef Martin Petersen.

SKIPPERLABSKOVS
captain's stew

Serves 8 ■ Preparation: 30 minutes ■ Cooking: 2½ hours

Ingredients

1 kg stewing beef, such as chuck

80 ml (⅓ cup) vegetable oil

4 onions, cut into 1 cm-thick slices

2 tablespoons red wine vinegar

500 ml beef stock

3 tbsp thyme leaves

2 dried bay leaves

1.5 kg floury potatoes, peeled

Chives and chive flowers (optional),
    to garnish

Cut the beef into large pieces, about 2.5 cm chunks. Season well.

Heat the oil in a large, deep saucepan over medium–high heat, add the beef and fry, turning, for 8–10 minutes until golden brown all over. Drain on paper towels. Add the onions to the pan and cook for 5 minutes, then deglaze the pan with vinegar and stock, scraping the base of pan. Add the thyme and bay, then return the beef to the pan and bring to the boil.

Meanwhile, cut the potatoes into 3 sizes, 500 g into 1 cm pieces, 500 g into 2 cm pieces, and the final 500 g into 4 cm pieces. Add these to the stew. Bring to a simmer, partially cover with a lid and cook for 1½ hours. Stir well and cook for another 1 hour. The meat should be tender and the majority of the potatoes should have mashed into the cooking juices, thickening the stew, and the larger potatoes should just keep their shape.

Serve in bowls with a knob of butter in the centre and garnish with chives, chive flowers if available and Pickled Beetroot (page 100).

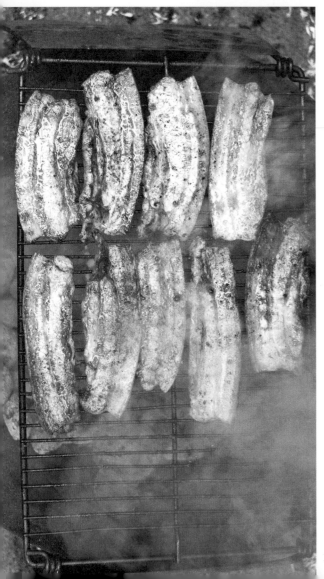

This could be the national dish of Denmark – the country is divided on whether the strips of pork belly should be fried or grilled. Samina Langholz has her own version – she prefers to cook it over a charcoal grill until tender and crisp.

STEGT FLÆSK
pork belly with potatoes

Serves 6 ▪ Preparation: 30 minutes, plus 20–30 minutes standing ▪ Cooking: 45 minutes

Ingredients

1 kg pork belly, cut into 1 cm thick slices

NEW POTATOES WITH PARSLEY SAUCE

1 kg small new potatoes

10 g butter

2 tbsp plain flour

350 ml whole milk

1 large bunch of curly or flat-leaf parsley

Arrange the meat in a single layer on a baking tray and season both sides. Leave for 20–30 minutes at room temperature. Meanwhile, light a charcoal barbecue and bring it to medium-high heat, making one side of the grill hotter than the other so you can move the meat to the cooler side if the charcoal is burning too quickly.

Put the potatoes in a large saucepan, cover with water, bring to the boil and reduce the heat to a gentle bubble. Season with salt, then cook for 20 minutes until tender. Drain, reserving the water.

For the parsley sauce, melt the butter in a small saucepan and stir in the flour. Over low heat, gradually stir in the milk. Return to the boil, stirring until thick. Add three-quarters of the parsley and 100 ml of the reserved potato water to thin the sauce down. Cover and set aside.

Place a grill rack over the charcoal. Put the pork over the hot part of the charcoal. Cook for 3–5 minutes on each side. The pork should be quite crisp around the edge. Serve with the potatoes and parsley sauce.

Every Dane has a strong opinion on how to get the best crackling. But it's generally agreed that you need to cut grooves deep through the rind into the fat and rub it liberally with salt. For added flavour, add a few bay leaves and stud the length of the rind with cloves.

FLÆSKESTEG
pork roast with crackling

Serves 8 ▪ Preparation: 30 minutes, plus overnight standing ▪ Cooking: 1½ hours

Ingredients

1.5 kg pork chop joint, with bones still intact, and the rind scored at 5 mm intervals

2 tbsp fine salt

8–10 dried bay leaves

20–24 cloves

2 large carrots, onions or parsnips, or 4 celery sticks, for roasting

3 apples, cored and sliced into 8 wedges

12 small red onions, halved

50 g butter

A splash of red wine or red wine vinegar

2 tbsp plain flour

350 ml pork or vegetable stock

Pat the meat dry. Rub the skin liberally with salt, then rub salt all over the outside of the meat. Insert bay leaves at regular intervals in the score marks along the rind, then stud the 2 outer edges of the rind with cloves. Chill overnight.

The next day, preheat the oven to 220°C (425°F). Place the pork rind-side down, in a shallow flameproof roasting pan and pour in enough hot water to submerge the rind, about 2cm in depth. Cook for 30 minutes.

Reduce the oven temperature to 180°C (350°F), then remove the meat from the pan and flip over. Set aside with the rind-side up. Place the roasting vegetables in the centre of the roasting pan, making sure the vegetables are slightly higher at one end. Place the meat on the vegetables, the smaller part of the joint on the higher pile of vegetables. Return to the oven and start timing. It will need to cook for 20 minutes per 500g (about 1 hour for a 1.5 kg joint).

Remove the pork and leave to rest on a chopping board. Discard the roasting vegetables. Put the apples, onions and butter in a large ovenproof frying pan and roast in the oven until tender. Meanwhile, place the roasting pan on the stove. Add a splash of wine and stir to deglaze the pan. Slowly add 100–200 ml stock and leave to reduce slightly. Add salt if necessary. Strain the gravy and serve with the pork and the apple and onion.

Mia Christiansen, sous chef at Barr, tells us one of the secrets to a succulent schnitzel is the brining of the meat. This is optional, but worth the effort. A basic brine is 1 litre of water mixed with 100 g salt, lightly crushed allspice, black peppercorns and a bay leaf.

BARR SCHNITZEL
with butter sauce

Serves 4 ▪ Preparation: 30 minutes, plus 2 hours brining (optional) ▪ Cooking: 15 minutes

Ingredients

SCHNITZEL

5 x large pork tenderloins (140 g each),
   brined for 2–8 hours
100 g (1⅔ cups) panko breadcrumbs
50 g (⅓ cup) plain flour
2 egg whites, beaten with a fork
Clarified butter and oil, for deep-frying

BROWN BUTTER SAUCE
200 g butter
2 lemons, segmented and chopped
50 g anchovies, cut into 1 cm pieces
1 French shallot, finely chopped
50 g capers, soaked in hot water for 10 minutes

PEAS, CHIVE OIL & VINAIGRETTE
220 g cold-pressed rapeseed oil
50 g apple cider vinegar
35 g white wine vinegar
15 g coarse mustard
1 g curry powder
1 g cayenne pepper
5 g Tabasco
2 g soy sauce
200 g fresh peas (peeled weight)
1 quantity of Chive Oil (page 92)

For the peas, blend the oil, vinegars, mustard, spices and soy for 30 seconds. Marinate the peas with the chive oil and vinaigrette and season.

Pat the meat dry, then cut each piece through the middle (not all the way through) to open out the tenderloin. Place between 2 sheets of baking paper and flatten with a meat mallet to 6–8 mm.

Blitz the panko breadcrumbs in a blender for 10 seconds. Coat the schnitzels in the flour, then in the egg white and then in the panko. Heat enough clarified butter and neutral oil for deep-frying to 170°C (340°F) in a large, deep frying pan. Fry the schnitzels for 2 minutes on each side until golden. Drain on paper towels and season with salt.

For the sauce, slowly heat the butter in a pan to 170°C (340°F), stirring. Once caramelised, cool to room temperature before straining through muslin.

Just before serving, heat the butter to 75°C (167°F). Add the remaining ingredients and cook gently for 3 minutes. Serve the schnitzel topped with the brown butter sauce, peas and Horseradish Cream (page 98), if liked.

The modern Copenhagen cook still likes to create that feeling of hygge at home, but the ingredient combinations are cleaner. They're still warm and inviting, just not as starchy as it once was. The finishing touches of horseradish, parsley and dill are the perfect complements.

WINTER SOUP
with chicken & kale

Serves 6 ■ Preparation: 1 hour ■ Cooking: 1½ hours

Ingredients

1.5 kg whole chicken

2 celery sticks, or lovage

1 onion, halved

1 bundle of herbs, including 2 bay leaves,
　6 thyme sprigs, and 4 parsley sprigs,
　tied together

1 tbsp whole black peppercorns

1 tbsp salt flakes

TO SERVE

2 leeks, sliced

225 g celeriac, diced

2 starchy potatoes, boiled in their
　skins and cooled, peeled and sliced

225 g cavolo nero, cut into 5 cm strips

Shredded horseradish, chopped dill and flat-leaf
　parsley and extra-virgin olive oil, to serve

Put the chicken in a large saucepan and cover with 3 litres water. Bring gently to the boil, skimming the surface. Reduce the heat and add the celery, onion, herbs, peppercorns and salt. Stir, and simmer for 1 hour or until the juices of the chicken run clear when the chicken is pierced through the thickest part (between the thigh and body). Cool, then remove the chicken and set aside. Strain the stock through a sieve lined with muslin, discarding all the flavourings.

Shred the chicken, discarding the skin and bones.

Just before serving, return the stock to the heat, add the leeks and celeriac and cook for 15 minutes. Stir in the potatoes and kale and cook for 5 minutes until the vegetables are tender. Adjust seasoning if necessary.

Divide the chicken between large shallow bowls and add ladlefuls of stock and vegetables. Serve with shredded horseradish, chopped dill and flat-leaf parsley, extra virgin olive oil and sea salt flakes.

La Banchina is located in an up-and-coming area known as Refshaleøen. Cooking is kept simple as the facilities are basic. They also forage and use the herbs found around the local coastline.

ALFRESCO DINNER
oven-baked salmon

Serves 4 ■ Preparation: 45 minutes ■ Cooking: 30 minutes

Ingredients

GARLIC CREAM

300 ml double cream

4 garlic cloves, bruised and skins removed

PARSLEY OIL

200 g flat-leaf parsley, including the stalks, coarsely chopped

200 ml neutral oil

SALMON

800 g salmon fillet, pin-boned, skin left intact

60 ml (¼ cup) olive oil

500 g Swiss chard, trimmed

15 g beach herbs, such as chickweed or orache (optional)

Preheat the oven to 180°C (350°F).

For the garlic cream, combine the cream and garlic in a saucepan and heat gently for 10 minutes. Remove from the heat and leave for at least 30 minutes to infuse. Season to taste. Reheat just before serving.

For the parsley oil, process the chopped parsley and oil in a blender for 10 minutes. Strain into a bowl or jug.

Place the fish on a large baking tray, season and drizzle with three-quarters of the olive oil. Cook for 20 minutes until just tender and still pink in the centre. The fish should flake very easily.

Heat a large cast-iron frying pan to medium–high heat, drizzle with a little of the remaining olive oil, add half the chard and cook for 3–5 minutes until just wilted. Remove and cook the rest of the chard. Divide the fish among 4 plates, breaking it into large flakes. Add the Swiss chard. Spoon over the garlic cream, discarding the whole garlic. Drizzle over some of the parsley oil and top with beach herbs.

Urban farming

Even though the countryside is not that far away from Copenhagen and many locals own small allotments on the outskirts of the city, there is still something special about reaching out of your window on the second floor and cutting some fresh parsley or going up on the rooftop and picking some fresh tomatoes. Urban farming has exploded in Copenhagen. As in many other cities, locals use every available space, from rooftops and balconies to public areas and courtyards. All you need is a sunny spot.

Plaice is the most common flat fish served all over Denmark. It can be breaded, fried and served on bread for smørrebrød. Here, the whole plaice is cooked simply in a mixture of extra-virgin olive oil and butter, then served with a caramelised lemon butter and potatoes.

STEGT RØDSPÆTTE
pan-fried plaice

Serves 2 ∎ Preparation: 10 minutes ∎ Cooking: 20–25 minutes

Ingredients

2 x 350 g whole plaice (or flounder), cleaned

2 tbsp rye flour

2 tbsp extra-virgin olive oil

100 g unsalted butter

2 lemons, cut into 5 mm-thick slices

2 tbsp chopped flat-leaf parsley

Boiled new potatoes, to serve

Pat the fish dry with paper towels, then season well. Put the rye flour on a plate and use to coat the fish, shaking off any excess.

Heat the oil in a large frying pan over medium–high heat, add 25 g of the butter, then once melted and sizzling, add the fish. Cook for 5–8 minutes on each side until the skin is crisp and the flesh is clean white. Remove the fish and place in a warm oven while cooking the second fish. Add another large knob of butter to the pan and cook the second fish.

At the same time, melt the remaining butter in another pan and add the lemon slices. Cook for 5 minutes until the lemon slices are browned on both sides. Add the parsley.

Place each fish on a plate and spoon over the lemon slices, parsley and butter. Serve with boiled new potatoes.

From September to April, mussels are at their best – plump and sweet. Many mussels are now farmed, which means cleaning them is easier. Make sure any live mussels that are still open when tapped are discarded, as they are dead.

MUSSELS
with onions & kale

Serves 4 ▪ Preparation: 30 minutes ▪ Cooking: 30 minutes

Ingredients

25 g butter

2 large onions, halved and cut into 5 mm slices

150 ml dark sherry

2 kg mussels, scrubbed and hairy beards removed

250 ml (1 cup) crème fraîche

350 g cavolo nero

Sourdough bread, to serve

Melt the butter in a large, deep saucepan with a tight-fitting lid over medium heat. Add the onion and cook for 10–12 minutes until starting to brown. Add the sherry and leave to bubble for 3 minutes. Add the mussels and stir with the onions and liquid. Cover and steam for 10 minutes, stirring once.

Open the pot, add the crème fraîche and toss again. Place the kale over the mussels and cook for another 5 minutes until wilted. Remove and discard any mussels that have not opened.

Divide the kale and mussels among 4 serving bowls. Taste the sauce and season if necessary. Ladle the broth over the top and serve with crusty sourdough bread.

There is a delicious trend in Copenhagen that has been happening for at least 5 years now, where vegetables and meat are heavily charred in a cast-iron frying pan.

CHARRED LEEKS
with almonds

Sreves 4 ■ Preparation: 30 minutes ■ Cooking: 20–25 minutes

Ingredients

4–8 leeks, depending on how thick they are

1 heaped tbsp krydderfedt (pork dripping)

50 g raw almonds, roughly chopped

2 tbsp fermented red wine vinegar (page 124)

100 ml crème fraîche, skyr or fresh goat's curd

Cut the leeks in half lengthways, right through to the root, leaving the root intact; this will hold the leeks together. Wash the leeks well and pat dry.

Heat a large cast-iron frying pan or large flat grill pan over high heat. Once it is super hot, place the leeks in a single layer, cut-side down, and cook for 3–5 minutes until the leeks are charred brown, almost blackened.

Flip the leeks over and reduce the heat to medium. Season the leeks and cook for another 2 minutes then add the pork dripping. Cook for 5 minutes until the leeks are softened. Remove leeks and set aside.

Add the almonds to the pan juices and toast, tossing occasionally, for 3–5 minutes. Add the vinegar and stir to release the bits on the surface of the pan. Spread the crème fraîche, skyr or goat's curds on a large plate and place the leeks on top. Spoon over the pan juices and almonds, then sprinkle with sea salt.

This recipe uses the whole cauliflower, making a purée from the florets and crisp vegetable shavings from the inner stem. Serve this dish as a side for stews or roasted fish.

CAULIFLOWER
with lemon & pumpernickel

Serves 4 ▪ Preparation: 30 minutes ▪ Cooking: 15 minutes

Ingredients

1 large cauliflower (about 350 g),
   green leaves removed

100 ml whipping cream or crème fraîche

Finely grated zest and juice of 1 lemon

50 g pumpernickel breadcrumbs (page 158)

50 g finely shaved parmesan

2–3 tbsp extra-virgin olive oil

Separate the cauliflower into florets. Trim the large inner stem from the vegetable in one large piece and set aside. Cook the florets in boiling salted water for 15 minutes until very tender.

Using a mandolin, finely slice the inner stem. Place in a bowl of iced water and chill until required.

Drain the florets, reserving a little of the cooking water. Purée the florets in a food processor or high-speed blender with the cream or crème fraîche until smooth, adding a little of the reserved cooking juices if necessary. Season with lemon juice, salt and pepper.

Spread the purée over a shallow bowl, top with the pumpernickel crumbs, parmesan, some of the lemon zest and half of the oil. Top with the crisp shaved cauliflower (drain it first), then drizzle with remaining oil and scatter with remaining lemon zest.

Small potatoes are the main staple in Danish cooking, and when the new crops arrive with their creamy yellow texture they are top of the list to serve at every meal, from the most simple to the most complicated, such as frikadeller, Wiener schnitzel or roast pork.

NEW POTATOES
with herbs

New Potatoes with Lovage

Serves 6 ■ Preparation: 30 minutes
■ Cooking: 15–20 minutes

Ingredients

500 g new potatoes

1 tbsp salt

2 large lovage or flat-leaf parsley sprigs

Place the potatoes in a bowl and add the salt, then rub them well with your hands, scrubbing the skins until the potatoes are well salted. Transfer to a large saucepan of water, add the lovage and bring to the boil. Cook until tender to the bite, but still slightly firm. Drain and return to the pan to steam dry. Slice large potatoes in half and leave small ones whole. Season and serve warm or cold.

Fried Potatoes

Serves 4 ■ Preparation: 20 minutes
■ Cooking: 30–40 minutes

Ingredients

500 g new potatoes

30 g salted butter

Cook the potatoes in a large pan of boiling salted water until tender. Drain and allow to cool. Cut small potatoes in half and large potatoes into 2.5 cm pieces. Heat the butter in a large frying pan, add the potatoes and cook for 10–15 minutes until crisp, golden and caramelised in places. Season.

Potatoes with Cream & Dill

Serves 4 ■ Preparation: 20 minutes
■ Cooking: 25 minutes

Ingredients

500 g new potatoes, peeled

25 g salted butter

200 ml crème fraîche

25 g finely chopped dill

Cook the potatoes in a pan of boiling salted water for 20 minutes, then drain and cut them in half lengthways. Melt the butter in a large frying pan, add the potatoes, season, then add the crème fraîche and mix until the potatoes are coated. Season, then fold in the dill. Serve warm.

Porridge or grød is the closest the Danes come to a risotto. They don't use rice but instead make the most of the grains they have on hand – barley, oats and wheat. This recipe is more of an autumn porridge with mushrooms and chard. Adapt the vegetables to the season.

BARLEY & MUSHROM GRØD

Serves 4 ▪ Preparation: 40 minutes ▪ Cooking: 30 minutes

Ingredients

1 litre chicken or vegetable stock

350 g mixed seasonal mushrooms, such as shiitake, chestnut, chanterelle, king, oyster and beech, sliced if large and stems finely chopped

2 tbsp grapeseed or sunflower oil

1 large onion, chopped

225 g pearled barley

100 ml dry white wine

75 g Vesterhavsost or parmesan cheese, finely grated

25 g unsalted butter

150 g mixed baby Swiss chard or beetroot greens

Pour the stock into a saucepan and bring to a simmer.

Heat the oil in large, deep frying pan and cook the onion for 5–8 minutes until tender. Add any chopped mushroom stems and cook to just soften. Add the barley to the pan and stir to coat, then add the wine and leave to bubble for 2–3 minutes. Stir in 2 ladles of the stock and cook, stirring, for 5 minutes. Keep adding stock, a few ladlefuls at a time, until almost all of it is used and the barley is tender; the barley will take about 25 minutes to cook, and should still be a touch nutty to the bite. Season, then remove from the heat and stir in the cheese. Cover and leave for 5 minutes.

Meanwhile, melt the butter in a large frying pan and cook the sliced mushrooms over very high heat until golden and just softened. Stir in the greens and cook until just wilted. Uncover the porridge and stir, adjusting the seasoning with salt if necessary. Add a little more stock if it's too thick, it should be loose and creamy. Spoon the mushrooms and greens over the top and serve with extra cheese.

SPECIAL
OCCASIONS

Christmas and New Year are big celebrations for all Danes.
Christmas Eve is the main Christmas dinner, and usually includes
roast duck, goose or pork belly, depending on family tradition. Easter
is marked with gravlax. In the summer, barbecues are lit at the first
sign of sunshine and everyone is out grilling pork and seafood – any
excuse to be outside. On the longest day of the year, bonfires are
lit on the coasts and people gather to celebrate.

The Danes are good at making the most of the outdoors, be it at the beach, or the local woods and fields, especially when the sun is out. This recipe can be used for mussels, cockles (vongole), prawns and crayfish. Fennel and seafood are excellent partners.

CLAMS
with fennel & parsley

Serves 6 ■ Preparation: 20 minutes, plus 30 minutes standing ■ Cooking: 30 minutes

Ingredients

2 kg small clams, such as cockles or mussels

2 tbsp rye flour

2 tbsp sunflower or grapeseed oil

1 onion, coarsely chopped

2 fennel bulbs (about 350 g), thinly sliced

150 ml dry white wine

250 ml (1 cup) crème fraîche

4 tbsp chopped flat-leaf parsley

Sourdough bread and butter, to serve

Rinse the clams then place them in a large bowl of ice-cold water and mix in the flour. Leave at room temperature for 30 minutes. Lift the clams up with your hands and wash again. Any clams that remain open after being tapped on a bench should be discarded. Store in the fridge until needed.

Heat the oil in a large deep frying pan with a lid over medium heat. Add the onion and fennel and cook, stirring, for 8–10 minutes until soft. Increase heat to high, add the clams, then the wine, and stir well. Once the liquid is bubbling, cover the pan and cook for 10 minutes. Stir, add the crème fraîche, stir to combine, and cook, covered, for another 10 minutes until the clams open. Discard any that have remained closed.

Stir the clams again, taste and season. Sprinkle with parsley and serve with sourdough bread and butter.

Cucumber is embraced by the Danes and has pride of place in many dishes. Here, the fresh taste of cucumber is complemented by peppery nasturtium flowers and leaves.

CUCUMBER SALAD
with nasturtiums

Serves 6 ■ Preparation: 25 minutes, plus 40 minutes standing ■ Cooking: none

Ingredients

1 English cucumber

3–4 Lebanese cucumbers

1 tbsp fine sea salt flakes

2 tbsp red wine vinegar

2–3 tbsp extra-virgin olive oil

2 tbsp chopped dill

2 tbsp chopped flat-leaf parsley

50 g nasturtium leaves

180 g thick Greek-style yoghurt

6–8 baby cucumbers with flowers,
   if available

6–8 nasturtium flowers

Cut the English and Lebanese cucumbers into quarters lengthways, then chop into 1.5 cm pieces. Place in a colander and sprinkle with the salt. Toss well and leave over a plate to drain for 30 minutes.

Wash the salt off the cucumbers and pat dry with paper towels. Transfer to a bowl and add the vinegar, oil, dill and parsley. Toss well and taste, adding salt if necessary. Leave for 10 minutes.

Toss the nasturtium leaves into the cucumber mixture. Spread the yoghurt on the base of a large serving plate. Add the cucumber salad and spoon in any juices from the bowl. Garnish with the baby cucumbers with flowers and nasturtium flowers.

*The revivial of Danish cooking and the great
movement of modern Nordic cooking means
that the Danes believe in seasonal cooking.
Elderflowers, for instance, are in season from
late May to mid-June. Surprisingly, elderflower
complements the rich flavour of mackerel.*

GRILLED MACKEREL
with elderflowers

Serves 4 ■ Preparation: 25 minutes ■ Cooking: 16 minutes

Ingredients

4 x 225 g whole mackerel, cleaned

125 ml (½ cup) extra-virgin olive oil

2 lemons, halved lengthways and sliced

100 g elderflowers

Vegetable oil, for brushing

80 ml (⅓ cup) red wine vinegar

TOMATO SALAD

2 large red heirloom tomatoes, sliced

4 medium green heirloom tomatoes,
    such as green zebra, sliced

2 tbsp extra-virgin olive oil

2 tbsp red wine vinegar

3 tbsp chopped flat-leaf parsley

2 tbsp chopped dill

Rub the fish with salt and pepper, then lightly rub with olive oil. Stuff each cavity with the lemon and some of the elderflower. Tie the fish at regular intervals with kitchen string.

Make the tomato salad. Arrange all the tomatoes in a shallow bowl. Season and drizzle over the olive oil and vinegar. Leave for 10 minutes, then sprinkle with the chopped herbs.

Preheat a charcoal grill to medium. Place the grill rack over the charcoal and leave to heat up. Brush the grill with vegetable oil. Place the fish over the charcoal and cook for 8 minutes on each side until charred and cooked through. Mix the the vinegar with the remaining olive oil and season. Place the fish on a serving plate and drizzle over some of the oil mixture. Garnish with extra elderflowers if liked and serve with the tomato salad.

Shrubs or drinking vinegars are refreshing and non-alcoholic. They are perfect to enjoy on a summer evening with friends. Adjust the sugar depending on the ripeness of the fruit. If you're using rhubarb, which is very tart, you will need to use the full quantity of sugar.

FRUIT SHRUB
seasonal

Makes 350ml ▪ Preparation: 20 minutes, plus 26 hours standing & 1 week fermenting ▪ Cooking: none

Ingredients

200 g caster sugar

2 lemons or oranges, zest cut into strips

250 ml organic apple cider vinegar with 'mother' or raw apple cider vinegar

FLAVOUR OF YOUR CHOICE

250 g elderberry blossom or flowers OR

1 kg fruit, such as rhubarb, berries, peaches, nectarines or cherries, stoned if necessary OR

100 g mint, lemon verbena or fresh ginger slices

Put the sugar and citrus strips in a large bowl. Muddle a little, cover and leave at room temperature for 1 hour.

Remove the citrus from the sugar and discard. Depending on the flavour you are making, add the elderberry flowers or fruit, herbs or ginger, then muddle to release some of the juice. Cover and chill for 24 hours.

Add the vinegar and muddle again, mixing well. Stand for 1 hour at room temperature, then strain through muslin into a screw-top glass jar or bottle. Squeeze the muslin well to release all the juice. Seal with a lid and leave to ferment in the fridge for a week.

To serve, dilute 15 ml shrub concentrate with 100 ml soda or sparking water, adding ice, if liked.

Gravlax is traditionally served at Easter as well as Christmas. The classic herb is dill with lemon zest. The modern touch is to add raw shredded beetroot to the cure. On slicing the beet-cured salmon, you will have a deep red colour followed by the orange of the salmon.

GRAVLAX 2 WAYS
modern & traditional

Serves 8–10 ▪ Preparation: 30 minutes, plus 48 hours curing ▪ Cooking: None

Ingredients

2 x 500 g pieces skin-on organic salmon, both
  cut from the centre of the fish, pin-boned

75 g flaky sea salt

75 g golden caster sugar

1 tsp roughly cracked black peppercorns

8 juniper berries or coriander seeds,
  lightly crushed

20 g chopped dill or coriander

1 large beetroot, peeled and coarsely grated
  (optional) or finely grated zest of 2 lemons

2 tbsp aquavit, gin or vodka

Pat the salmon dry with paper towels and set aside.

Put the salt, sugar, peppercorns and juniper berries in a bowl with the herbs and mix well. This is the 'cure'.

Line a large baking tray with plastic wrap, still attached to the roll. Place the first piece of salmon on top, skin-side down. Add beetroot or lemon zest to the cure mix, rub the cure on the fish, then drizzle over the alcohol of your choice. Top with the other piece of salmon, skin-side up.

Wrap the salmon sandwich tightly with plastic wrap. Place a heavy saucepan flat on top of the fish to weight it down and refrigerate for at least 48 hours, turning the fish over every 12 hours. The longer you leave the fish, the more it will cure. Four days of curing is good. To serve, unwrap the fish, brush the cure off with kitchen paper, then very thinly slice the fish at a 45-degree angle.

JULEAND
slow-roast duck

Serves 8 ∎ Preparation: 45 minutes, plus 20 minutes resting ∎ Cooking: 4½–5½ hours

Ingredients

4–5kg duck or goose

1 tbsp fine salt

1 tbsp freshly cracked black pepper

500 g fragrant apples, cut into wedges, about 1.5 cm thick

3 French shallots, halved

100 g prunes

15 g thyme sprigs, plus extra to serve

1 tbsp grapeseed or sunflower oil

ROASTING VEGETABLES

2 large carrots, quartered, cut into 7 cm pieces

2 large onions, thickly sliced

2 large celery sticks, cut into 7 cm pieces

1 tsp sea salt flakes

GRAVY

150 ml port, sweet vermouth or dry red wine

40 g unsalted butter

40 g plain flour

Remove the fat close to the cavity of the duck. Wash the duck and pat dry. Rub all over with half of the salt and pepper. Stuff the front cavity (at the neck) with some of the apples, then bring the flap of skin over the apples and secure with a toothpick.

In a bowl, mix the shallots, prunes, thyme, remaining apples and some of the remaining pepper. Place in the large cavity. Rub the duck with oil and rub with remaining salt and pepper. Tie the legs together and pin the wings to the side of the bird with 2 metal skewers. Place on a wire rack over a tray and chill to dry out the skin, up to 24 hours.

Preheat the oven to 120°C (250°F). Bring the duck to room temperature. Place the roasting vegetables in the centre of a roasting tray and place duck on top. Sprinkle with a little more salt. Roast for 4–5 hours. The inner temperature should be 80°C (176°F). If the pan is getting dry, add 150–300 ml water.

Rest the duck on a board and set the vegetables aside. Pour the juices off into a bowl and leave somewhere cold for the fat to set on top, then spoon the fat off. You should have at least 350 ml duck juices. If not, make up with water.

Place the roasting pan over low heat and add the port to deglaze, scraping well. Add the butter to melt, stir in the flour, then the duck juice. Cook until the gravy thickens. Serve the duck with the gravy and vegetables, garnished with thyme.

This recipe is traditionally made for Christmas. Peeling the potatoes takes a long time, but it can be done in advance, and the cabbage can be braised up to 2 days ahead. Reheat just before serving and serve with the slow-roasted duck for Christmas dinner.

THE TRIMMINGS
potatoes & red cabbage

Caramelised potatoes

Serves 8 ▪ Preparation: 1 hour
▪ Cooking: 30 minutes

Ingredients

1 kg new potatoes

100 g sugar

50 g lightly salted butter

50–75 g duck fat, for cooking

Cook the potatoes in a large saucepan of boiling salted water for 15 minutes until just tender, but not cooked all the way through. Drain and cool, then peel off the skins, pulling rather than cutting.

Add the sugar to a large heavy-based frying pan in a thin even layer and melt slowly without stirring. Once melted and caramelised to a light golden colour, add the butter and a little duck fat, if liked. When bubbling and sizzling, add the potatoes and coat with the butter. Cook, turning, for 15 minutes until golden brown and caramelised. Season well and serve.

Braised Red Cabbage

Serves 8 ▪ Preparation: 20 minutes
▪ Cooking: 1½ hours

Ingredients

1 whole red cabbage, about 1kg

80 ml (⅓ cup) red wine vinegar

2 strips orange zest

2 strips lemon zest

1 tbsp allspice, lightly crushed

1 cinnamon stick

50 g unsalted butter, diced

Olive oil, to serve

Preheat the oven to 150°C (300°F). Cut the cabbage into quarters and remove the inner core. Thinly slice the cabbage, then place in a large ovenproof saucepan with the vinegar, citrus zest, allspice and cinnamon. Season, then dot with the butter.

Crumple up a large piece of baking paper, wet with cold water, then open out and place over the cabbage. Cover with a lid and braise for 1½ hours until tender. Stir and adjust the seasoning if necessary. Drizzle with olive oil, if liked.

Oysters for New Year's Eve

The flat, wide Pacific oyster is the most common species found in the Danish Wadden Sea. Oysters are available through the year, but are especially good with Champagne for New Year's Eve. Here are some topping ideas.

Redcurrants

Tops 8 oysters

Mix 1 finely chopped French shallot with 2 tbsp redcurrants, mashing the redcurrants to release their juices. Season, spoon onto the oysters and finish with a string of chilled redcurrants.

Rhubarb Vinaigrette

Tops 12 oysters

Cut 1 large rhubarb stalk into tiny dice. Place in a bowl with 1 small diced French shallot, 2 tbsp red wine vinegar, salt and a pinch of sugar. Lightly crush ¼ tsp coriander seeds and add to vinaigrette. Leave for 10 minutes. Spoon onto oysters to serve.

Lumpfish Roe

Tops 8 oysters

Finely dice 1 French shallot and mix with the juice of ½ lemon. Season to taste, then add to oysters. Top with lumpfish roe and colourful herbs.

Cucumber & Nasturtium

Tops 12–16 oysters

Peel 1 Lebanese cucumber and finely dice. Place in a bowl with 2 tbsp pumpernickel oil or parsley oil and 2 tbsp apple cider vinegar. Stir, and season to taste with salt. Spoon over the oysters and top each with a nasturtium leaf or flower depending on the season.

Cucumber & Horseradish

Tops 12–16 oysters

Peel 1 Lebanese cucumber and finely dice. Mix with 2 tbsp grated horseradish, 2 tbsp sunflower oil and 2 tbsp apple cider vinegar. Stir, and season to taste with salt. Spoon onto oysters and sprinkle with black pepper.

This traditional New Year's Eve cake is made with marzipan. It's a series of rings, of which there are typically at least 5 layers, but you can increase the amount if you like. The almond rings can be made up to 3–5 days ahead and kept in a cool place until needed.

KRANSEKAGE
new year's eve cake

Serves 8–12 ■ Preparation: 40 minutes, plus 1 hour chilling ■ Cooking: 12–15 minutes

Ingredients

200 g almond meal

70 g plain flour

400 g caster sugar

½ tsp ground cardamom or cinnamon

300 g egg whites, beaten with a fork

1 kg marzipan, grated into large shreds
   and chilled

ICING

300 g icing (confectioners') sugar

3–4 tbsp water or milk or lemon juice

1 handful of dried cornflowers, to decorate

Combine the almond meal, flour, sugar and spice together in a mixer. Add half the egg white and mix, then add the marzipan, mixing to make a paste, adding as much of the remaining egg white needed to bind the dough. Bring the dough together, cover, and chill in the fridge for 1 hour.

For the icing, sift the icing sugar into a bowl and gradually mix in the liquid. The icing needs to be thick. Put in a piping bag and set aside.

Preheat the oven to 190°C (375°F).

Divide the dough into 8-9 different-sized pieces (or the traditional 4–6). Using damp hands, make several ropes, all 4cm thick, but different lengths. For example, make one rope 8 cm long, one 12cm long, another 14cm, 16cm, 20cm, 24cm, 26cm, 28cm and 32cm, etc. – this will create a series of rings in different sizes. Bring the ends of each rope together to form a ring, then place on 2 large baking trays lined with baking paper, spaced well apart. Roll the small piece of leftover dough into a ball.

Bake for 12 minutes or until golden. Remove the rings and ball and cool completely.

To assemble, pipe a zigzag of icing on each ring and allow to set, Layer the rings in order, largest at the bottom and ball at the top. Decorate with dried cornflowers. Serve at midnight on New Year's Eve.

Recipe list

Index

Suppliers

BREAKFAST/COFFEE CAFÉS

ANDERSEN & MAILLARD
Nørrebrogade 62
2200 Copenhagen N

+45 30 86 49 22
http://andersenmaillard.dk

APOLLO BAR
Charlottenborg
Nyhavn 2
1051 Copenhagen K

+45 60 53 44 14
http://apollobar.dk

GRØD
Jægersborggade 50, basement
2200 Copenhagen N

info@groed.com
https://groed.com

You can also buy some of the freeze-dried berries toppings here.

THE COFFEE COLLECTIVE
Headoffice,
Godthåbsvej
2000 Frederiksberg C

+45 60 15 15 25
https://coffeecollective.dk/da/

They have various locations throughout the city.

LUNCH

ØL & BRØD
Viktoriagade 6
1620 Copenhagen K

+45 33 31 44 22
http://www.ologbrod.dk

RESTAURANT PALÆGADE
Palægade 8
1261 Copenhagen K

+45 70 82 82 88
https://palaegade.dk

GASOLINE GRILL
Landsgreven 10
1300 Copenhagen K

https://www.gasolinegrill.com

SCHØNNEMAN
Hauser plads 16
1127 Copenhagen K

+45 33 12 07 85

http://www.restaurant
schonnemann.dk

HOT DOGS

HANEGAL
Organic sausages

http://hanegal.dk/forhandlere/

JOHN'S HOTDOG DELI
Flæsketorvet 39
1711 Copenhagen V

https://kodbyen.kk.dk/artikel/
johns-hotdog-deli

RESTAURANTS

ADMIRALGADE 26
admiralgade 26
1066 Copenhagen K

+45 33 33 79 73
http://www.admiralgade26.dk
restaurant@admiralgade26.dk

AMASS
Refshalevej 153
1432 copenhagen

+45 43 58 43 30
www.amassresturant.com

BARR
Strandgade 93
1401 Copenhagen K

+45 32 96 32 93
https://restaurantbarr.com

GRO SPISERI
Æbleøgade 4, rooftop
2100 Copenhagen Ø

+45 31 87 07 45
www.grospiseri.dk

LA BANCHINA
Refshalevej 141
1432 Copenhagen K

+45 31 26 65 61
https://www.labanchina.dk

SPISEHUSET 5C
slagterhusgade 5c
1715 Copenhagen V
en grå kødby

+45 28 93 68 79 (Torsten)
https://food8.dk/spisehuset/

BAKERIES/CAKES/SWEETS

HANSEN IS
https://hansens-is.dk

JUNO
Århusgade 48
2100 Copenhagen Ø

https://www.instagram.com/juno_
the_bakery/

KARAMELLERIET
Handmade caramels
Jægersborggade 36
2200 Copenhagen N

+45 70 23 77 77
http://karamelleriet.com

LECKERBAER
Ryesgade 118
2100 København Ø

+45 28 40 48 64
leckerbaer.dk

LILLE BAGERI
Refshalevej213B
1432 Copenhagen K

https://lillebakery.com

OLUFS IS
Olufsvej 6
2100 Copenhagen Ø

+45 27 59 38 36
http://www.olufs.dk/

WINTERSPRING DESSERT
Dessert bar, artisan ice cream
 & cakes
Store strandstræde 16
1255 Copenhagen K

+45 30 47 77 88
www.winterspringdesserts.com

WINE BARS

SABOTØREN
Fensmarksgade 27
2200 Copenhagen N

+45 21 32 00 19
www.sabotøren.dk

VED STRANDEN 10
Ved stranden 10
1061 Copenhagen K

+45 35 42 40 40

VEXEBO WINE
Danish produced natural wine
Veksebovej 9
3480 Fredensborg

www.vexebovin.dk

VINHANEN
Baggesensgade 13
2200 Copenhagen N

+45 29 92 14 52
www.vinhanen.dk

OTHERS

Butchers

SLAGTEREN VED KULTORVET
Frederiksborggade 4
1360 Copenhagen K

+45 33 12 29 02
https://www.kultorvet.dk

Spices
https://www.asaspice.dk

You can also buy dried blue
cornflowers here

Wild food/herbs mushrooms, etc.

THOMAS LAURSEN
http://wildfooding.com

Cheese

OSTEN VED KULTORVET
Rosenborggade 2
1130 Copenhagen k

+45 33 15 50 90
http://www.ostenvedkultorvet.dk

Smoked fish/seafood

HASLE RØGERI
www.hasleroegeri.dk

NORDBORNHOLMS RØGERI
https://nbr.dk
https://shop.nbr.dk

Herring

CHRISTIANSØPIGENS SILD
Info@christiansoe-pigens-sild.dk

Liquorice

https://lakridsbybulow.dk
Liquorice candy

https://www.matas.dk/helse-
sundhed/foedevarer-slik-snacks/
slik-snacks/lakrids

Raw and some sweets

Waffles/bottom for making 'flødeboller'

https://www.urtegaarden.dk/
floedebollebunde-45-mm

Food market

TORVEHALLERNE
Frederiksborggade 21
1360 Copenhagen K

www.torvehallernekbh.dk

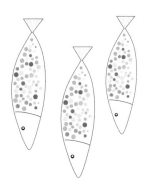

Acknowledgements

Thank you to everyone in Copenhagen who made this project possible – the chefs, cooks and our friends and family who gave us their family recipes as well as their versions of classics, traditional and modern classics. Thank you also to The lab and Emil who made it possible. Our assistants were the best – Morten Bentzon for taking up this challenges and patiently guiding Christine with all technical stuff, Karen Moltesen and Amalie Gielow for organising all our props and Katrine Meilke on food. Thanks to Adam Engel who also stepped in for a few days. They ran around the city with us, helping to catch Copenhagen at its best. It was hot, (amazing summer of 2018) and everything was even more delicious. Thanks to Cecilie Svanberg and Jesper Laier who helped us with the early steps and helped shaped the book. Then thank you to Catie Ziller (publisher), Kathy Steer (copy-editor/editor) and Alice Chadwick (design) for your patience to get to the finishing line.

COPENHAGEN WE LOVE YOU!

Published in 2019 by Murdoch Books, an imprint of Allen & Unwin
First published in 2019 by Marabout

Murdoch Books Australia
83 Alexander Street, Crows Nest NSW 2065
Phone: +61 (0)2 8425 0100
murdochbooks.com.au
info@murdochbooks.com.au

Murdoch Books UK
Ormond House, 26–27 Boswell Street, London WC1N 3JZ
Phone: +44 (0) 20 8785 5995
murdochbooks.co.uk
info@murdochbooks.co.uk

For corporate orders and custom publishing contact our business development team at salesenquiries@murdochbooks.com.au

Authors: Christine Rudolph & Susie Theodorou
Photographer: Christine Rudolph
Illustrator: Tusnelda Sommers
Cover Illustrator: Michelle Tilly
Design: Alice Chadwick
Editor: Kathy Steer
Food stylist: Susie Theodorou
Assistant food stylist: Katrine Melike
Assistant: Adam Engel
Photo assistant: Morten Bentzon
Props assistant: Amailie Gielov & Karen Ravnsbæk Moltesen
Props stylist: Christine Rudolph
Ceramics & tabletop by: Janaki Larsen, Gurli Elbækgård

Publisher: Corinne Roberts
Cover designer: Madeleine Kane
English-language editor: Justin Wolfers
Production director: Lou Playfair

© Original edition 2019 by Marabout

Christine Rudolph, born and raised in Copenhagen, is an international interior stylist, set designer and photographer. Christine has lived in Melbourne, Australia, working with *Vogue Living* and *Donna Hay*, and also in New York. Now back in Copenhagen, Christine has a small workshop–studio in the middle of the city and is involved in numerous interiors styling projects, including curating the ceramics for the new Noma 2.0 restaurant.

Susie Theodorou was born and raised in London. She is author of numerous cookbooks and a culinary stylist in UK and the USA. She has collaborated often with Christine Rudolph and has been excited to collaborate again in a celebration of Copenhagen's trending yet timeless cuisine.

ISBN 9 781 76052 473 9 Australia
ISBN 9 781 91163 231 3 UK

A cataloguing-in-publication entry is available from the catalogue of the National Library of Australia at nla.gov.au
A catalogue record for this book is available from the British Library

Printed in China by C&C Offset Printing Co. Ltd.

MIX
Paper from responsible sources
FSC® C008047